THE LOVE PROJECT WAY

We delight
in walking the
Way of Love
Diane F. Pike
Arleen Lorrance

1/81

THE
LOVE PROJECT WAY

by
ARLEEN LORRANCE
and
DIANE KENNEDY PIKE

LP Publications, P.O. Box 7601, San Diego, California 92107

Illustrations are by Diane Kennedy Pike, with the exception of that on page 136, which is by Leslie Shelton.

Printed in the United States of America

First Printing, September, 1980

Published by LP Publications, 1980
The Love Project, P.O. Box 7601, San Diego, California 92107

*Typesetting and Photo Offsetting by Center City Printing
1031 - 14th Street, San Diego, California 92101*

Library of Congress Cataloging in Publication Data

Lorrance, Arleen, 1939-
    The Love Project way

    1.   Conduct of life   I.   Pike, Diane
Kennedy   joint author.   II.   Title.
BJ1581.2.L693   241   80-36806
ISBN 0-916192-15-6

This Book Is Dedicated To

*All Who Seek to Walk the Way of
Universal Love*

ACKNOWLEDGMENTS

This book represents an accumulation of shared knowing gathered from seven years of constant interaction with **Seekers** all across the country and in other parts of the world. We are grateful to all who have practiced alongside us as we have been applying the **Love Project** principles in our own lives and as we have shared them with others. Our own growth in our ability to be universally loving, and our understanding of the process involved in unfolding into universal consciousness and into universal loving, have been enormously enhanced by other **Seekers'** willingness to risk and to share, to trust and to explore.

We are especially grateful to the twelve California **Seekers** — Ron Podrow, Millie Boucher, Sid Stave, Anne McLaren, David McLaren, Carl Downing, Dottie Wiles, Elsie Daly, David Daly, Anita Pitcher, Lucille Barru, Milly Collinsworth and one other — who were will to share explicitly in chapter nine of their life experiences and their practice of the **Love Project** principles; to Leslie Shelton for her illustration on page 136; and to Millie Boucher for her help with proofreading.

THE
LOVE PROJECT WAY

CONTENTS

INTRODUCTION

This is a book about how to *be* the power of universal love in your life every day. It offers a way to go beyond *believing in* love to *knowing* it through your own experience; beyond wishing you had love to bringing it to life in you.

To admire love is not enough if you do not know how to *be* loving. To be universally loving is to be open, to give *and* receive. It is to live in joy, to delight in life, to be filled with energy, to look forward to each new moment. To be loving is to live in higher and wider consciousness, to bring spiritual wisdom into everyday engagings, to see the larger meaning of seemingly simple events, to live as a Master Incarnate, expressing all of your energies in life-affirming acts, in harmony with the perfect pattern of the whole. All this is to *be* the power of love.

Wherever you are on your own path of unfoldment, this presentation can be of help to you. If you are well on your way in each of the regards described above, this is your opportunity to go even further. If you are just beginning, this will help you to remain centered in your Essential Self while you stretch beyond your heretofore self-imposed limitations into the larger you that is evolving.

If you are a doubter, a cynic, a fatalist—one who has lost faith in the power of love—this book might offer you a fresh look. You might come to see that what you actually rejected was your own narrow view of love and that that very view needed to be doubted, needed to die, in order that you might build a larger, less disappointing, less limited perspective. Indeed, it is our hope that you will find in these pages very specific ways to activate the love force in your life that will surprise *even you*—surprise you enough to enable you to let some of the patterns you've chosen to live by be replaced with ones you haven't yet dreamed of.

If you are a novice and are just beginning to seek your own unique way of being an agent of love in the world, this book can help you to build a firm launching pad.

1

This is a guide book on *how* to love. The "how" rests upon a definition of love. To be conscious of what love is *to you* is to become conscious of the specific ways and means of actually bringing that love into being.

We would like to offer a working definition of love as *unblocked, free-flowing life energy.* To block energy is to hold back, cause congestion, and eventually create conditions of dis-ease. To block energy is to stop the life flow, to inhibit and constrict, to invite the breakdown of the energy fibers in which you live and have your being. To block energy is to say "No" to life in the form it comes to you, to cut yourself off from other persons, to isolate yourself in a prison of distrust.

To allow energy to flow freely in all circumstances and with all people is to live in harmony, to say "Yes" to life, to open the door to never-ending growth, to unite in spiritual oneness with the self you have always been and yet have sought desperately to know. All of this awaits you when you learn to love.

Love is the binding quality of the life force—that cohesive dynamism that causes opposite polarities to be drawn to one another, that enables the life current to leap from the negative to the positive poles (and vise versa) so that new life, new force, new power is released. Love is that which enables us to communicate with one another, the living membrane that connects our individualizing units of consciousness, the ocean of oneness that disenables us from becoming islands unto ourselves.

It is the nature of the life force to be loving—to flow uninhibited thoughout the 'body'* of time-space-substance that we call 'this world', or the universe. That life force flows in and through each of us and 'connects' us with all that is and all who are. The only way we can be *un*loving is to interfere with that flow, to block the life energy as it comes to us or seeks to flow through us. When we block our energy flow, we cut ourselves off and begin to go 'dead' within our own energy fields. To the extent we succeed in blocking the flow, to that extent we are unloving.

---

*Throughout we use single quotes to indicate words used metaphorically or as a manner of speaking, without a precise referent in the dynamic energy reality.

2

This is a book about how consciously to unblock your life force and let it flow uninhibited through your energy field, thus *being* the power of love in your life. The "how" is presented in the form of six simple principles known as **The Love Project.** The principles are as old as time, as young as they are new to you, as workable as you make them, as profound as their application. **The Love Project** principles are a way of life, a path of unfoldment, a vehicle for journeying into self, a means of making love work.

The Love Project principles are:

- *Be the change you want to see happen, instead of trying to change everyone else.*

- *Receive all persons as beautiful exactly where they are.*

- *Provide others with the opportunity to give.*

- *Perceive problems as opportunities.*

- *Have no expectations, but rather, abundant expectancy.*

- *Create your own reality consciously, rather than living as if you had no control over your life.*

REMEMBER: *Choice is the life process. In every moment of awareness, you are free to make a new choice.*

We will be exploring them in depth in the pages that follow. Since 1970 persons have been using these principles to facilitate the cosmic unfoldment of their lives in consciousness and to enable them to be actively loving in the world.

These six principles of love may be for you. Knowing that, it is our joy to offer them to you as an expression of the love force which they represent.

3

Chapter One
THE COMING OF THE PRINCIPLES

The Love Project principles are a practical way of applying ancient wisdom to daily life. They are principles to *practice* rather than talk about, a way of life rather than a philosophy or religion, a form of action as differentiated from prayer. They serve to awaken the inner wisdom *in* the Seeker rather than urging that Seeker to follow another's path, or worship one reported to be more enlightened than self.

The principles came into being in an action-oriented way, accompanied by very specific projects through which to implement them. They were tested *as* they evolved. They came in the form of doings devoid of ritual. Their sacredness was in their facilitativeness, their truth in their results.

The Love Project principles are life-transforming. In this regard, it is highly appropriate that they were given to and through one who had made the conscious choice to transform her life—Arleen Lorrance.

"Prior to 1968 I was an energetic, high-powered, ambitious, creative, achieving individual with an insatiable desire to be loved, a highly active temper, and a great fear of risking and of being hurt by others. I was a staunch agnostic, knowing without question that I didn't know if a higher source existed. I had grown up tough in a Brooklyn ghetto without benefit or limitation of religious orientation. I was not really looking for anything beyond the bounds of myself, but I *was* pushing myself to the perimeter of my consciousness and to the limits of my physical stamina.

"In May, 1968, my transformation began. Stricken with heart disease, I was given six weeks in bed followed by six months of limited activity—what seemed an eternity of time—in which to start anew, open my heart center, express gratitude for life, and take baby steps in a new direction. In August-September, 1969, I broke through to Cosmic Consciousness. I saw through the darkened glass into the Light of the awareness that I am all there is and nothing at all.

"Having experienced my complete oneness with all there is, I began devouring books and studying materials in a crash course of reminding myself of the ancient wisdom I had always known but had hidden behind the back of my overpoweringly-expressive personality self. I had not remembered that my Higher Self knew well how to enact wisdom in life on this plane.

"As a result of past-life recalls which enabled me to make new choices about who I wanted to become based on an eye opening view of who I *had* been, I made the commitment to becoming totally loving, vulnerable and open. This commitment was a signal to a waiting universe that another of its children was ready to channel—to bring into being yet another unique expression of the 'one truth' that always was and ever will be.

"Following my conscious commitment to being totally loving, vulnerable and open, I was taken to classes in my sleep over a period of about a week and a half. Each night I went to the same classroom. Though persons-in-form were not present, energy-beings who were recognizable from night to night were. As morning approached I was conscious of easing myself through levels of consciousness until I returned my awareness to the physical plane. I awoke knowing that what I had learned in my sleep was the most profound material I had ever encountered. Yet, I could not remember *any* of it. I realized that the instruction was taking place on one plane and I was awakening on another, so I didn't push myself. One night I was taken to a classroom 'farther back,' 'deeper in,' a longer way down the 'hallway.' It was clear I was ready for the More, and it was given.

"Then the instruction ceased. The classes came to an end. I waited, alert as to when and how what I had learned might come into being on this plane of consciousness. The day came not too much later. A fight broke out in the auditorium of the ghetto high school in which I was teaching. Someone had to intercede. I knew I was being asked to see if I was fully ready to bring in what I had learned. I went forth without question or hesitation, bringing the power and force of love through my presence. I knew no fear: perfect love had cast it aside. I served as a conduit of peace in what could have been an arena of bloodshed.

5

"Trembling from the concentration of life energy that had plummeted through me, and drenched from the flood of tears that had been shed before my class as we had talked of the event and its implications, I returned to my office—a devotee to the cause of love, committed to finding a way to bring harmony to our battered school environment.

"I sat down, and all at once there was in my office a ray of light illuminating the six principles of the **The Love Project** and showing me how they could immediately be put into practice in the school. I knew that these principles were what I had learned in my 'sleep school,' and that now I was ready to see them because I had proven I was ready to *be* them.

"Without a moment's hesitation, **The Love Project** began at Thomas Jefferson High School. Within a seven-month period the principles, practically applied in a series of Love Projects, helped to transform the school from a place of violence and negativity to a center of love and caring.*

"**The Love Project** principles came to life in real life situations. They were not for anyone *else* to do but for *me* (for each of us) to do. They were not for me to proselytize about or even to convince others of their value. They were for me to live. They became apparent through my example, not my salespersonship."

The Love Project principles are transformers, enabling persons to *create new realities* consciously through the configuration and reconfiguration of energy.

"'T ·vas able to rechannel my energy and high power into areas of service that went beyond my own desires. My ambition fell away as I actively and ecstatically fulfilled my lofty dreams for 'tomorrow' in the miraculous activity of the now moment."

The Love Project enables persons to *be the change they want to see happen instead of* dropping the seed of their creative urge upon the ground in the futile act of *attempting to get others to change* to meet their image of how a situation should be.

"*Being the change* heightened my use of my creativity beyond my wildest dreams. I was able to bring more into'being than ever before, to achieve to a far greater degree than in any

---

*See *The Love Project*, by Arleen Lorrance, LP Publications 1978, (Revised Edition).

previous period. The **problems** at the high school that had previously engulfed me **became opportunities** for new growth for all who wanted it. The waters in which we had been drowning for lack of willingness to swim a new stroke, became the baptismal font of our birth into functioning as divine beings in manifested form.

"We **provided others with the opportunity to give,** and in so doing I personally came to know what it is to reach beyond the confines of my limited personality self into the larger Self—the oneness of which we are all part—the God Force which is not capable of being packaged and distributed by any one brand of religious production but *is* that which we all are when we are conscious that we are."

The Love Project principles enable persons to love unconditionally—not in theory but in practice—through *receiving all persons as beautiful exactly where they are.*

"I had had **no expectations** about what would come of the sleep travel instruction, but I had **abundant expectancy** that if I didn't push the river it would flow to me and I would see a way to ford it to new beginnings. When the principles were given I rejoiced, having **no expectations** about what or if they would accomplish or where they would go from their humble beginnings, or if they would be meaningful. Their impact on the ghetto high school was almost miraculous. Not only were individual lives transformed, but so was the spirit of the entire school.

"In time I went forth as a pilgrim, knowing I held divine wisdom in my awareness and boundless love in my heart. I left New York and my job as a high school teacher to find a new way to express love in the world. In my **abundant expectancy** I met Diane through a series of non-coincidental occurrences, and we were sent forth two-by-two in the work of being living examples of **The Love Project** principles in our own lives.

"We *are* a Love Project, as are you if you exemplify these principles in your own life. We are, all of us, a family—a family of love on a spiritual journey, acknowledging the perfection of now, being and doing our highest and best in the holy moments of every day."

The Love Project principles came into being to be practiced. May this book further facilitate that process for each of us.

Chapter Two
CREATE YOUR OWN REALITY CONSCIOUSLY

Create your own reality consciously is perhaps the most fundamental of the six **Love Project** principles. It is based on an inner knowing that all persons bring their own realities into being, but most are not conscious that the creational powers are theirs.

What we mean by "reality" is whatever is real to each individual. "Reality" in this sense, takes into account the fact that no 'external' or 'objective' reality can be known except from a particular point of view. The 'observer' participates in bringing the reality into being. There are many different levels on which we can recognize this principle of 'relativity,' first demonstrated in the physical sciences by Einstein and expressed explicitly and systematically in the realm of human sciences by Alfred Korzybsky in Modern Semantics.

Creating Visual Realities

On the level, for example, of visual perception, we know that light waves register on the retina and are transmitted via nerve impulses to the brain. It is in the brain that the nerve impulses are decoded and 'images' are formed. The image we 'see,' then, is not the object itself but our own creation in response to the object. We say we see things "as they are." In fact, we see, and then we give the form and shape of mental images to what we see. When we respond, then, it is to the images on our mental screens rather than to the energy itself, because our physical sense of sight is not able to transmit nerve impulses rapidly enough to enable us to see with our ordinary vision the molecular interaction which characterizes the energy reality of the world we live in. We function in relation to the closures we make which translate the energy into seemingly 'solid' objects, the 'things' we perceive.

8

A metaphorical example is what happens when we look at an electric fan before and after the current in turned on. When the fan is off, it is clear that it is comprised of several separate blades. When it is on, it whirls so rapidly that our nerve impulses cannot travel quickly enough to indicate to us the movement of each blade. Therefore, the image we form in our minds and thus 'see' looks like one solid disc, seeming to stand still. The fan is not structured differently because it is in motion, but we are unable to perceive its real makeup or structure. We fall back instead on our own approximation. We abstract the most predominate impulses received and form an image which looks like a solid metal disc.

So it is with the so-called 'material' objects in the world around us. As *we* see them, these objects are 'solid' and 'standing still.' In reality, they are swirling masses of vibrating molecules of energy which we could see only if our mechanism on the physical level were refined enough to register all the data. If the energy were 'standing still,' if the 'motor' were turned off, we would see it as individual molecules clustered together in patterns. When it is 'turned on,' or activated, however, the molecules are moving so rapidly that even with the aid of high-powered instruments that help extend our perception, we can see only the 'pathways' of their movement, which scientists call energy waves. With our ordinary physical sense of sight we see 'objects' that appear to be quite solid and relatively motionless.

Thus we create our own reality each time we look at any 'thing' with our physical eyes. We *learn* to see and identify objects, we learn to abstract. Our language is an important part of the process of decoding by which we form images that conform to our group reality, or cultural perceptions. Without words, we would not learn to identify, name and discriminate between various 'objects' and the colors and textures thereof. What is real to us, therefore, is what we have learned to identify as real, what we have learned to perceive.*

Linguists have found, for instance, that Eskimos learn to perceive and identify many different kinds of snow. They do not have a general word for snow as we do in English. They have names for many different 'objects' they perceive, all of

*Carlos Castenada's books are excellent examples of learning to see things differently by receiving different instruction and training.

which we group together under the one word 'snow.' What is real to them is a wide variety of different kinds of precipitation that falls in cold weather, which is their constant habitat. Their reality is quite different from ours.

In order to perceive something new, we have to have a name for it. The word enables us to give form and shape to the energy we are perceiving and to "tell" it from other energies. Most of us are conscious of the interaction between words and the ability to perceive from having learned to distinguish shades of colors. It is possible, for example, to see the color red and to include in that reality a wide spectrum of hues. If someone asks you to identify shades of red, however, you must have names to correspond to the limits you place on your perception. In that way, you include only those hues which correspond to that 'reality' you have learned to perceive. You can only distinguish between magenta and maroon because you have been taught to identify the hues, brightness and degree of saturation that characterize each.

We learn in just the same way to discriminate between all 'objects'—by learning words and fitting our perceptions to them. To learn several languages, therefore, is to have several different ways of perceiving the world, just on that most basic level of "naming" or "labeling" things, and beyond the basic level, there is the level of nuance: each language carries its own rhythm, timber and feeling-meaning to describe a given experience through a given word.

The reality we perceive, then, is once removed from our actual experience of it as energy. We perceive the image we create in response to our interaction with the energy field we say it represents. (The first order of abstracting.) The energy is. What we 'see' of it is our own creation. We give it its name and its definition. (The second order of abstracting.)*

Creating Emotional Realities

Another level on which we can be aware of the theory of relativity in action as we create our realities is that of emotional responses and preferences. For example, a whole

---

*For a further exploration of this whole theme, see Korzybsky's *Science and Sanity* and other works on the Science of General Semantics.

group of persons can observe the 'same' phenomenon and yet describe it very differently because of the emotional responses they evoked in relation to it.

Supposing you were to watch a football game with a group of friends, some of whom were for one team, others for the other, and still others had no team preference but either liked or disliked football as a sport. At the end of the game, all will have seen the same events, having learned to decode the energy configurations into images called 'football.' Those supporting the winning team may say that it was the best game they ever saw played. Those who rooted for the losers may say that it was a terrible game, poorly played, the referees were biased, the wind too strong, the teams inept. Those who enjoy watching football no matter who is playing may say that it was an exciting and thrilling game. Those who dislike football under any circumstances may say that it was boring as usual. All speak of the same event, but what is real to them is colored by the emotions they create in response to it.

The same goes for foods eaten, persons met, films seen, parties attended, lectures heard, classes enrolled in, jobs held, books read, persons met, etc., etc. Supposing, for example, you read a book on the best seller list because so many of your friends have raved about it as fantastic, exciting, one of the best ever written. You may find the book uninteresting, poorly written and contrived. It is the same book, but what it was for you differed enormously from what it had been for many others. How good is the book "really"? It is as good as it seems to each person who reads it. The book is. The emotional responses and preferences created in response to it are pure reality creations.

Creating Meanings and Values

Another level on which we create our own realities is in the meaning and value we attribute to things. You are signed up to go on the same foreign tour with several other persons. The trip is cancelled. For you, the cancellation is a confirmation that you are not intended to travel. "Every time I make plans to go somewhere, something happens so that the plans don't work out. I have never travelled outside my home state. Obviously

I'm not intended to." For another person, the cancellation opens the door to new adventure. "Since I can't go with that group, I guess I'll strike out on my own. I've always wanted to travel in foreign countries. I will take three months instead of three weeks and bum around Europe on my own. It'll be more of a challenge and less expensive." A third person responds, "Oh, well, I didn't care much whether I went or not." A fourth person is furious. "I saved my money, put in a special request for my vacation at that time, told my friends and family I was going. They can't do this to me. I will demand reparations. They have ruined my whole year. I will certainly never do business with them again!"

The illustrations could go on, but the point is made. The event is the same, but each person attributes to it a different meaning. To some its value was far more intense than to others.

Or, several students receive 'A' grades on a history exam. One feels he got what was coming to him, since he had studied so hard. For another is was a confirmation of how lenient the teacher is, since he knows he could have done much better. Still another feels lucky, since she didn't have time to study at all. You are simply relieved. Your parents had said you couldn't go to the school dance unless you got an A on the test. The grade is your 'ticket' to the dance. Nothing more.

For the parents of the students, the value of the grade varies from the most important indication of how intelligent their child is, to having no significance at all. "It's just another test grade. So what?" To the teacher the grades are an indication of her teaching and test-making abilities. For the school counselors and administrators, the grades will help determine whether the student passes or fails.

The grades have no value in and of themselves. They just are. Any value attributed to them is pure reality creation by the persons involved.

Or, you and your wife are traveling on a bus with nearly forty other persons. A sniper, firing a rifle at random in the streets, hits your wife in the head with a bullet and kills her instantly. Some of your friends assure you that your wife had some karmic debt to pay—that's why she, and no one else, was hit. Others indicate that surely God singled you out to be saved because you have an important work to do; otherwise the bullet would have struck you, since you were sitting right next to your wife. Others say this is divine retribution on you (or your wife) for past sins. Others say you are being given an opportunity to witness to the power of love and forgiveness in the world. Others that the act was senseless, meaningless, revealing that there is no justice in the world, no hope, no way to live in peace.

In fact, the incident was neither devoid of meaning nor was it limited to any one meaning. The event itself holds the potential for any or all meanings to be abstracted from it. What you choose as the meaning *you* see in it is your reality creation. If you are conscious of that fact, you can choose the one you feel will be most beneficial to you and to others.

Morals and ethical standards are values attributed to certain kinds of behavior. In order to *do* what is right, we must first determine what *is* right and what is wrong. These values are not inherent in the behavior. For example, in the United States school system, on the whole, we have decided it is wrong to "cheat." Then we define "cheating" so that people will know what not to do. Two definitions for cheating are copying from another's paper during a test, and giving someone else an answer you know to a question being asked of the other. On the other hand, in a South American country familiar to the authors, "cheating" by copying from another's paper is not seen as wrong, but rather as "vivo" which means smart, sharp or clever, and giving someone an answer he needs when he is put on the spot or letting someone copy your answers while doing a test is seen as an act of friendship and love. No one who is a friend would deny information to another who needs it. The latter has nothing to do with cheating; it has to do with being a good and loyal friend. In this case, values are almost completely reversed. In our culture it would be wrong to give the answer to another; in the other culture it would be wrong not to.

It is because the moral or ethical values are not inherent but rather are attributed to an event or a pattern of behavior that moral standards can change. In our society, for example, there are several long-standing moral codes which are currently (1980) being challenged, debated, re-evaluated and changed.

Not too many years ago, divorce was considered evil, a sin, or at the very best a terrible failure to be succumbed to only in

13

humiliation, and most state laws permitted it only under the most severe of circumstances (proven adultery or extreme cruelty on the part of one spouse against the other), and even then it took a long time to process. Now, more and more states are making it relatively easy to get a divorce in a minimal amount of time. This is because fewer and fewer people see divorce as wrong. Rather, it is coming to be seen as an alternative open to people just as marriage was an alternative they chose earlier. And along with the alternative of divorcing, that of not marrying at all but simply living with someone is also opening up. Not too long ago that was completely taboo, and those who lived together without marrying were seen as living in sin. Now they are seen by many as experimental, risking, open.

Or take abortion. Abortion used to be a considered so horrendous an act that it created extreme guilt and shame in those who chose—most often against the law—to terminate a pregnancy. Now more and more people feel that the woman has the right to decide whether or not to bring a pregnancy (in its early stages) to full term. Whether an abortion is 'right' or not is more and more frequently left to the woman and her doctor to decide.

Likewise, war used to be seen as a sign of patriotic bravery and a display of a nation's strength. Today, more and more people are coming to see war as foolhardy, futile, terribly risky and even evil. So much is this moral question in flux as to whether or not to go to war to kill a so-called "enemy" that it is possible within one family to have one son who is a career naval officer, one who is willing to go to jail rather than to cooperate in any way with a system of conscription that gives the decision-making power over his life to his government, and still another who is willing to serve his country but not to kill, and who thus does alternative service as a conscientious objector.

All of this is by way of saying that *we* create the values, morals and ethical standards that guide our behavior, and we are free to alter those standards whenever we wish. Our choices are our own reality creations, even when we choose to accept the predominant values in our culture because of the great social pressures put upon us to do so, or when we adopt 'belief' systems that reinforce certain values by attributing 'evil' and 'good' to them and offering a system of rewards and punishments in the after-life to keep us in line.

Creating Realities Through Action

Another level on which we create our own realities is in what we do and don't do. If you go out on the streets, for example, smiling and saying hello to persons, you will probably experience the world as friendly. Persons will probably smile back, greet you in return, welcome you into their day. If you share of what you have and are with others, if you tell people how much you love and appreciate them, if you open the doors of your home and heart to others, more than likely you will feel you are living in a world of abundance and love, a world in which affirmation and sharing surround you and fill you just as they flow out from you.

If, on the other hand, you complain a lot, criticize persons constantly, wear a frown, do not give to others because they do not give to you, and invite few if any persons into your home and heart, you will probably experience life as miserable, unhappy, lonely, unfulfilling and difficult, the world as hostile and people as untrustworthy.

What you do and do not do determine how you experience life. If you do not do anything meaningful with your life, you will probably experience life as dull, routine and meaningless. If you spend your efforts in service to others, in active support of causes you find worthwhile, you will probably feel that something is happening in the world to make it a better place to live, that things are changing and forces are moving to bring hope to persons in need. We are the agents of our own reality creation in that whatever we are doing, or not doing, is the most active impression made upon our own consciousness. We determine to a large extent what we see happening in the world around us because what we see most clearly is what *we* are doing.

Moreover, in doing what we do, we naturally become affiliated with others who are similarly involved. Persons acting on behalf of similar causes generally band together to make their efforts more effective. If you take an interest in hospital care by becoming a volunteer assistant, for example, you will quickly discover how many other persons there are who care enough to volunteer their time in such an effort. If you sit home, doing nothing but complain because no one does anything about improving hospital care, your own lack of activity reinforces your conviction, for you are exposed to no one but yourself, and you don't care enough to do anything.

If it is your habit to drive faster than the speed limit of 55 mph, you will find yourself competing on the freeways and turnpikes with other persons who are also exceeding the speed limit. "You see?" you may say to yourself, "no one obeys the law any more." If, however, you go 55 mph yourself, you will be surrounded by other persons who are going your speed and you will be conscious of how many people *do* obey the law, and how those who speed past you stand out as "lawbreakers," the few among the many. The more serious your own infractions of the law become, the more conscious you will be of other lawbreakers, and the more you will live in 'their world.' If you never break a law, on the other hand, you may find yourself unable to believe that anyone would, and thus be shocked by the behavior of those who get arrested for infractions of varying degrees of seriousness.

These examples point up another facet of how what we do and don't do helps to create our realities. What we do tends to draw to us a like energy output from others and persons who are functioning out of similar energy. Persons who are friendly and outgoing, who speak first to others, extending their interests and concerns and sharing of themselves and their own life experience, usually have many friends. Persons are friendly to them in return; they share back, showing an equal concern for the one who reached out. Thus, those who already have lots of friends seem to get more and more, adding abundance to what was already sufficiency.

On the other hand, persons who are withdrawn and insecure, reluctant to speak to others because of uncertainty, and who share little of themselves because they are not certain how they will be received, tend to have few friends and to feel that few persons really care about them or reach out to them. Others feel as awkward with them as they were afraid they would, and thus their fears and insecurities are reinforced. What we send out is more often than not what we get back, and in this way we draw to us experiences which complete the reality we have set in motion from within.

Persons who are fearful, distrusting others, worrying that they will be victimized, often have their fears confirmed. Those who are trusting, open and unafraid, seldom have experiences which would cause them to change their orientation to life. The energies we send forth draw to us those energies which will make them whole. We help fulfill our own prophecies by generating and initiating the energies which will bring our own futures into being.

Creating Realities Through Habits

Still another way we create our own realities is through habit patterns. Habits can be formed on many different levels. If you form habit patterns of activity, for example, you create for yourself a reality of predictability that may make your daily life organized, efficient, and easy to maintain because you know in advance just what to do in order to have things go as you want them to go. However, your daily life may become terribly dull—so routine that boredom sets in and overtakes your zest for life. Moreover, if you live in habit-patterned motions, anything that interrupts your routine may be experienced as threatening, anger-producing, hostile, irritating, annoying or even mentally and/or emotionally disturbing. You will have created a reality for yourself of repetition and sameness which will be safe and secure, because it demands nothing new of you in each new day, but also risky, because in reality everything changes each day and sooner or later you are likely to be rudely confronted with the fact that you have not stayed current with that change.

Or, let's say you have formed a habit pattern of going to church each Sunday. In your reality, it may seem that "everyone" goes to church on Sunday, because that behavior is all you know. You see the world through your own patterned behavior, as through a grill over a window. What does not fit your pattern does not exist as far as you are concerned.

Such a reality is safe and comfortable until the day when someone you know and love, perhaps one of your own family members, one of your children, does not conform to your patterns. You are forced to recognize their behavior as different, but because you have so restricted your interaction with life that you have left no room for a deviation from that pattern, you find yourself being upset, judgmental, worried, frustrated, feeling a failure, etc. You do not really open yourself to what your loved one *is* doing, so focused are you on what he or she is *not* doing. You may even think/feel that he/she is doing this *to* you, so personally does it offend you, whereas in fact, he/she may simply be making choices out of his/her own reality.

We all form emotional patterns which create our realities. Often these patterns are repetitive responses based on events in our childhood. Suppose, for instance, you were born to an authoritative, strong-willed parent who, without apparent regard for your preferences, ordered you around. You sustained a sense of your own integrity by obeying your parent while lashing out in anger at other persons. Now, as an adult, you resent instructions given to you by any person who has authority over you—even those anonymous persons who put up traffic regulation signs or write the instructions for filling out application forms. "Who are they to give me orders and boss me around?" you fume. You *do* follow instructions, carry out your job, etc., but you find yourself lashing out in anger at perfect strangers at the slightest provocation, often surprising yourself at your vehemence. Or you find that you have no patience with your spouse and children, "flying off the handle" for "no reason at all." Your reality is that (a) persons are always bossing you around, and (b) people do things just to make you angry—even strangers. In fact, however, you are simply perceiving and responding to the world through the grid of emotional habit patterns formed when you were small, and through those patterns, you recreate the same reality over and over and over again.

Or, when you were very young, your mother and father both died in an auto accident. At the time you felt abandoned. The only two persons you had ever been close to "left" you without so much as a word of explanation or even a leave-taking. As the years went by, you grew to love your grandparents, who were raising you as if they were your parents. Then in your critical teen years, both of them died within two years of each other. Once again you felt abandoned. You created the reality on a feeling level: "Whoever I get close to, whoever loves me and whomever I love, leaves me, even if they have to die to get away."

As an adult, you find yourself unable to love or let yourself be loved for fear you will be abandoned. Whenever anyone begins to express love for you, you begin to distrust them, feeling they will hurt you deeply if they get the chance. Your experience is that the only way to be safe is never to love or be loved. Consequently, you are always alone and lonely, living inside the reality that you were indeed abandoned early in life and continue to suffer the consequences of that abandonment.

You feel life has dealt you a hard and cruel blow. In fact, you are merely re-creating a reality you first created as a small child and continue to create as an adult through an emotional habit pattern.

There are also mental habits—some of them enormously powerful. Take a very common one that could be labeled a "cause and effect" pattern. You were taught problem solving in school, and the pattern you learned was to look for the "cause"— that which brought the "problem" into being—in order to solve the problem by eliminating the cause. This pattern worked. extraordinarily well in solving the problems given you in school—problems that were designed to *teach* you to look for the 'cause' and then remedy it. Having found the pattern useful, you adopt it as an habitual response to life.

You are seated in a concert hall. The friend beside you responds to the magnificent music you are hearing with tears that fall silently down her cheeks. Suddenly you are distracted from the concert, for your mind is problem solving. "Why should she be crying now? Is something wrong? Did I say something to upset her on the way here? Is she sorry she came with me? Did something just happen to her and I was too insensitive to notice?"

In this situation there is no real problem—at least not that you know of. But your friend's unexpected response to a mutually-shared experience has triggered a mental pattern which takes over, pulling you out of the experience itself and into a mental exercise which, while helpful when problem-solving, is irrelevant when just being present to someone. More-over, it introduces reality creation such as, "She's keeping something from me," or, "She's impossible to understand," or "She's too emotional to cope with." In fact, all she did was to

19

shed a few tears in response to some very beautiful music.

In focusing on what the matter might be, you are creating the reality that something is indeed wrong. To ask, "What's happening?" rather than, "What's the matter?" is to inquire of your friend what her reality is, rather than superimposing your own on hers.

Or, you may have developed a mental pattern of finding fault with persons, events, situations and plans. Now you live in a reality of hopelessness, discouragement and depression, not realizing that it is your own mental habit pattern that disenables you from seeing the good in persons, events, situations and plans, and thus having reason to have hope, take heart, and feel good about life.

Creating Realities Through Life Experiences

Another way we create our reality is by the kinds of experiences we open ourselves to. If, for instance, you never open yourself to the possibility of experiencing anything except through the five physical senses of touch, taste, sight, smell and hearing, your reality will be that it is impossible to know anything except through these five senses. If persons tell you that they have seen things in advance of their happening, or have communicated on thought waves, or have experienced a wider reality of which we are all part, you will dismiss their sharings as impossible, or pure imagination. If, on the other hand, you are open to all possibilities, then you will not only listen with interest when persons tell you of experiences they have had that you have not, but you will open yourself to those experiences in order to see and know for yourself.

If you open yourself to experiences beyond the physical senses, but are convinced there is only "one way" to know a wider reality—through the grace of a given teacher or guru or savior, through following certain teachings or a prescribed path to enlightenment—then indeed for you there *is* only one way. You have determined your reality. Anyone who shares that they have found another way is of necessity wrong from your point of view.

We also help to bring our realities into being by the sounds we make and the words we speak. Sound is a creative force. Sounds have patterns of their own and arrange molecules according to their patterns. Consequently, the sounds we make with our creative instruments called voices, actually help to reinforce and sustain, and also to alter, our reality creations.*

Even the way we move our bodies and the way we hold our muscles help create our reality. A person living in constriction will usually hold onto his body and thus not only mirror that reality creation, but perpetuate it by what he is doing with his body. A lazy person, on the other hand, often sends little life through his body, and because the body has little life, it "does" little in life. If we would change a reality, we often need to work with changing the form and shape of our bodies, learning new walks, postures, skills, etc., teaching ourselves new physical habits, so that the new reality can be manifested wholly in our energy world.**

Living in Private Worlds

Thus we can see that there are a multitude of ways of creating our own realities. The process of doing so is enormously complex—and seems the more so because most of us create our realities *unconsciously*. As a result, our experience is that the reality is forced upon us by circumstances, by other persons, or even by our own feelings. We feel the victim of "the way things are" and not at all the creator acting out of total and perfect freedom. Moreover, because we do not know that we have created our own realities and continue to do so, and think that the way we experience life is the "way things are" in some objective sense, we assume that other persons see the world the way we do (or should), feel what we feel (or would if they allowed themselves to), have motives that fit what we perceive to be the cause of our troubles, etc., etc. In other words, we see the whole world through the colored glasses of our own reality creation without knowing that we have glasses on at all.

---

*See *Toning*, by Laurel Elizabeth Keyes, DeVorss, 1977.

**It is for this reason that so many physical approaches have arisen to help people discover their potential by releasing muscular tension. Reichian therapy, the Alexander approach, Rolfing, Polarity Therapy, Bioenergetics, massage, foot reflexology and many more are approaches which help people create new realities by altering physical configurations. Hatha Yoga and acupuncture are ancient expressions of the same truth.

As long as we are unconscious of ourselves as creators of our own realities, as long as we do not know ourselves to be the *power* with which we create the realities we live in, we are locked inside a private world, unable to get outside it to see things as they really are. We live with our own images of reality, the values we attribute to those images, the meanings we give to our experiences, the feelings we have about ourselves and others, our own thought processes. This private world is not directly responsive to the real energy world, but is abstracted from it. When we are locked inside it by our unconsciousness, we are disenabled from knowing life, ourselves and others, as we/they really are.

Perhaps a metaphor would be helpful. It is as though you were given a test tube (your personality self: higher self, objective mind, feeling self and physical body) in which to carry on life experiments to discover what it is like to be a creator. You carry on the experiments, but in the process you forget that you are the experimentalist and begin to feel/believe that you are the experimented with or upon. You feel it is all happening *to* you instead of that you are causing it to happen in order to understand how the 'chemical interactions' of human life work. Instead of expanding your sense of knowing and understanding in the course of your life experiments, therefore, you begin to feel more and more trapped, more and more at the mercy of inner and outer forces. You feel you *are* the test tube rather than the one who is carrying on experiments in this very mobile and adaptable scientific laboratory of earth experience.

When you have forgotten who you are, it is difficult to alter the initial experiments you set in motion. The chemical reactions will continue until that day you wake up and realize that you are the experimentalist and can design a new experiment, and introduce new 'chemicals,' at your will. Then your life experiences will begin to change and take on new qualities and new character.

The 'chemical reactions' set in motion by the original conceptual design you as experimentalist were working with at the outset of this lifetime are what is often called your unconscious mind. It governs your reality until you remember that you are able to change that reality at your own will. As long as you are unconscious of the *process* of reality creation, of the numerous ways you bring your life experience into being, of those 'chemical reactions' you have set in motion, you *are* the victim of your own past choices held in your unconscious mind as patterns of response, habits, etc. Thus, the first step toward consciously changing your reality and consciously creating new ones is to become conscious of the realities you have already brought into being and how you have managed to do that.

Observing Your Process Of Reality Creation

This requires activating your observer self—that aspect of your Higher Self which is always aware of what is going on in you at all levels. When you allow this observer self into your consciousness you begin functioning in stereo, so to speak. At the same time as you are interacting with another person or participating in an event, you are also watching yourself interact and participate.

You are, for example, involved in a conversation with a close friend. He begins to share with you about the difficulties he is having with his wife. You are listening to what he is saying and at the same time your observer self is reporting to you: my heart is racing and I have butterflies in my stomach, my hands are turning cold and sweaty, my head is starting to pound.

This is the beginning of becoming conscious of your own process of reality creation. You have allowed your awareness of what *is* happening in your private world, your little portable laboratory, to surface in your consciousness, even if you are not yet conscious of how and why it is happening. In the beginning, as you are practicing becoming conscious of your inner processes, you may want to say out loud what you are conscious of internally. You might say to your friend, "As you talk, I'm aware of my heart racing, of butterflies in my stomach, of my hands turning cold and clammy, and of my head starting to pound." (Please notice that you do *not* say, "You are making me feel....," for you are practicing being conscious that this is *your* reality creation, not someone else's.) If your friend says "Why?" or "What's going on with you?" simply respond, "I don't know," if indeed you do *not* know at that point.

When becoming conscious of your process of reality creation, it is important to practice staying with the observer self, which simply sees what *is*, and *that* it is, and never judges. If you slip into your rational mind and demand to know "why" before you have *seen* what's going on, or if you say, "This is ridiculous, I shouldn't be feeling this way," or "If my friend knew how I was reacting, he would never share with me again," you will cut off your consciousness of your process. Your censoring mind will push your awareness of your reality creation into your unconscious where you cannot make choices about it in freedom.

To say you shouldn't feel what you are feeling is not to change your reality, it is only to pass judgment on it. In order to *change* the reality (if that is what you want to do) you must know what it is and how you brought it into being to start with. That requires simple observation of what is, without judgment.

You may not want to interject your observations of your own process into your conversations with your friend. But if you don't you *will* want to report it later in the day, either by sharing it with a friend who will receive it nonjudgmentally, or by writing it down for yourself in a notebook or journal in which you record your inner processes. Generally speaking, if you only *think* about an awareness, it will get away from you rather quickly. To fix it in your consciousness, it is important either to write it out or to share it aloud with a friend. Then it will be yours to work with consciously.

Often, in the process of articulating your observations of your process, you will become aware of other aspects of your reality creation. For instance, you may discover thoughts that were running subliminally across your mental screen: "What if that were to happen to me? I couldn't handle it. I wouldn't know how to live without my wife. She's the center of my existence." Or, "I have many of the same feelings about my wife and our relationship, but I could never tell her. What would happen? And what would my family think?" Or, "He doesn't realize what a fool he's making of himself, talking like this. He should keep his private troubles to himself."

Write those thoughts down, too. Or share them with your friend, or your spouse. "Do you know what I found myself thinking while Jack was talking to me about his problems with his wife?"

24

Or, you may discover feelings you were not aware of before. Feelings of fear, panic, disgust, dislike, anger. Those are also parts of your reality creation. Verbalize them somehow so that you bring them fully into your consciousness.

Becoming aware of your process will enable you to be more conscious of the larger reality you are creating for yourself. In this case, your thoughts or feelings may be leading you step by step toward a crisis in your own marriage which could be averted if you would share what's going on in the early stages instead of waiting until you explode with the impact of what you have been building up unconsciously inside of you. As you articulate what is going on, you take charge of your reality creation and can make new choices if you want to. Also, you have an opportunity to do some reality checking with your wife to see what *she* is experiencing, what reality *she* is creating. In the process, both of you will gain clarity about the way you are relating to each other.

Suppose you are reading a good book. Suddenly you become conscious that you are experiencing tension in your back and shooting pains in your legs. Before moving and doing anything, let your observer self report exactly what's going on: "I was reading about those persons getting lost while hiking in the High Sierras. I felt tension in my back and shooting pain in my legs." Perhaps you make a note of that in your journal. Perhaps you tell your spouse or a friend.

The next day you are driving your car. Another car darts out from behind a parked car. You swerve and miss and in the next block, your observer self reports: "That car just missed me. I am feeling tension in my back and shooting pains in my legs." Again, you either record the awareness in writing or tell a friend.

After observing yourself in several situations in which you "find yourself" feeling tension in your back and shooting pains in your legs, you will begin to see a pattern. You might be able to say, for example, "When I am frightened, or fearful, I create tension in my back and shooting pains in my legs." Once you can see that this is the reality you *do* create (habitually) under certain conditions, then you can begin to change that reality if you want. When in a situation that is usually fear-producing for you, you can turn your conscious attention to the muscles and nerves in your back and legs. If you do not want to create tension and pains, you will concentrate on what you *do* want, and bring that into being. You might want to create relaxation and alertness, and therefore might practice deep breathing, both to keep your muscles relaxed and to bring in new energy with which to act, should action be called for.

Having been able to bring your physical responses to fear-producing situations into consciousness and having exercised choice to create a new reality, you may then want to turn to the fear, and bring that reality creation into consciousness. Practice listening to your observer self to see under what circumstances you create the feeling-response of fear. Having accumulated sufficient data as to what you *do*, decide if that is what you want to do. If not, then begin to make new choices in those situations. Create instead a reality of excitement, attentiveness, trust, willingness, or whatever you decide is the reality you *want* to live within.

Bringing your reality creations into consciousness, then, involves:
1) observing what, in fact, you do feel, think and do;
2) observing under what circumstances and in which situations you do what you do, feel what you feel, think what you think;
3) seeing that you choose those feelings, thoughts and actions in response to those situations and circumstances, they do not just "happen" to you.

Creating a new reality involves:
1) deciding you *want* to create a new reality;
2) recognizing that if you created the old one, you have the power to create a new one to replace it;
3) deciding what new reality you want to create;
4) practicing bringing the new reality into being whenever you are in circumstances or situations similar to those in which you used to create the old one.

The Higher Self

The observer is one of the roles or functions of the energy of Higher Self. Higher Self is that aspect of ourselves which is linked to the All, the Source of our being, "God." If we were to use other terminology for the Higher Self, we might call it God Within, the spirit, the soul, the Over-Self, the Higher Mind, the teacher within. Higher Self is the source of all our awareness, our consciousness, our life force, our wisdom, our knowing, our 'higher' will. It is the source, but only in a limited sense, for *its* source of supply is the larger Self of which it is a part—the One, the All. Each person is an individualizing expression of the God Force. The infinite Life Force becomes finite in each of us. The Higher Self is that aspect of ourselves which never loses touch with its divine origin, that knows who we are and how we can live in total peace, harmony and ease in this universe of which we are a part. Our Higher Selves know our perfect patterns and can reveal those patterns to us.

It is in Higher Self that you will find the freedom to create your own reality consciously. The rest of your personality self—your physical body, your feeling self (Little Self), and your objective mind—are mere reflectors. They reflect your state of consciousness and the choices you are making. Often you may be choosing merely to reflect realities being created around you because you are not conscious of any other possibilities. As your consciousness expands, however, you will begin to see the more that awaits you, and your physical body, feelings and thoughts will begin to reflect the perfect pattern held for you in the vastness of the All and caught for you, transmitted to you, by your Higher Self.

When you reflect the realities being created around you, you are not an active creative agent yourself, though you are exercising your power of choice to a limited degree by selecting *which* realities to reflect in yourself. You are, in this case, a participant in a group mind or psyche. Most of us function to a large extent out of this group psyche when we are children. What we do, feel and think is primarily a reflection of what the persons we live with do, feel and think. To the extent you were *different* from the persons around you, to that extent you were responding to your own Higher Self even though you may not have been conscious of doing so.

Therefore, even though you may have created a reality for

yourself—what you are "like," the "kind of person" you are—which is not entirely *original*, nevertheless it is *your* creation in that you determined from your Higher Self the particular combination of qualities and characteristics and modes of behavior you would select from your environment to make you what you are.

The Individualizing Process

You may observe yourself and see that you are like your mother in certain respects, like your father in certain other regards, like your general culture in other ways, and unlike anyone you know in some aspects of your personality. It is the combination of all these factors that makes you who *you* are. Your reality is utterly unique.

Until you become conscious that this is so, however, you may say, "It's my mother's fault that I am..." or, "It's my father's fault that...," not realizing that you chose whether or not to incorporate that trait into your character and how to think and feel about the qualities you saw in your parents—even *what* qualities to see in them.

If, for example, your parents were very prejudiced against people of other races, you may "find yourself" being prejudiced and say that it's their fault. However, if you look at your brothers and sisters, you may discover that one or more of them chose to be open to and understanding of other racial groups precisely because they recognized your parents' prejudice and did not want to mirror-reflect it. Others may never have noticed your parents' prejudice at all and therefore not have any consciousness of race. The opportunity to be prejudiced was there for all of you if you chose to reflect it. Some of you did, some of you didn't.

Or, your father may have been very dictatorial, demanding your conformity to his will. You may have responded to this by being dictatorial, too, in relation to all persons who are under your 'control'—family, spouse, employees, etc.—thinking that you came by it 'naturally' from your father. Another in your family, on the other hand, may have chosen to be weak-willed, unable to make decisions for himself, lacking in self-confidence. Another may have chosen to be rebellious against all authority figures, asserting her will

28

in opposition to others rather than for herself or anyone else. Still another may have chosen to seek ways to live and work cooperatively with others. Your father was being who *he* was being. Each of you responded to him as you chose. None of your realities were *his* fault, or *his* creation.

Or, you may have been raised with parents who were unable to express their love and affection directly, and who therefore never said "I love you," or held you, or kissed you, or touched you, or gave you positive feedback and verbal support. You, therefore, may say, "I am insecure and have low self-esteem because of the parents who raised me." Another person, however, raised by parents who also failed to express affection outwardly, may have grown up feeling sorry for his parents, having assumed the role of parent and nurturer toward them even as a child. Another may have developed a strong inner core of self-affirmation, knowing her own worth and giving herself the positive feedback she needed, thus becoming independent, self-reliant and strong. Another may have dedicated his life to service to other persons, *giving* them the love and outwardly warm affection and affirmation that he never received himself.

Family environment was only one of the influences in your growing years, even if the most prevalent in most cases. You were also raised in a particular culture (a culture being a group reality that is shared by many, many people to varying degrees), fell into a particular economic stratum of society, attended a particular school system or systems, belonged to a particular religious grouping, etc. In each of these cases, you were provided group realities to sample and you will have selected certain elements from those group realities to incorporate into your own private world.

We human beings as a species are evolving in our state of identification with group psyches, or realities. In our more primitive states, human beings were identified with small groups and had no sense of any reality beyond that of the group. There was no concept of "I". There was only "we". As our consciousness of self began to unfold, we also began to expand our sense of group identity from the small group (tribe or clan) to larger groupings of human beings, each more diverse than the last: states, nations, alliances of nations, Western civilization or culture, and Eastern civilization or culture, and even the planet as a whole.

29

In fact, in *very* recent times, some persons have begun to see the possibility of identifying with living beings different from human beings who live on other planets in this universe, and perhaps even in other universes.

At the same time as our sense of group identity has been expanding outward into ever larger and more diversified group realities, so has our sense of our own individuality grown, and our identity with, and eventually our freedom from, our own private worlds. It would appear that we are moving toward the day when each of us will consciously create a unique private world in which to live and have our being while understanding and acting out our oneness with, and therefore our need to cooperate and live in harmony with, all other living beings in the vastness of the cosmos.

The point here is that our environment and the circumstances of our lives provide us with opportunities for growth, for expansion of our consciousness. How we respond to those opportunities—whether we see them as problems and say "no" to them, or as challenges which we accept and learn from—only *we* can determine. That is how we create our own realities and is an expression of our uniqueness.

As you begin to become conscious of the reality you have been creating, therefore, you may want to look back over the events and relationships of your life to see what choices you made. What qualities did you choose to mirror-reflect in your personality that were present in persons you knew as you grew up? What habit patterns of interaction and living did you select out to help form your patterns of living? What values did you accept for your own? What values do you present to yourself as "shoulds" and "oughts" that remain unevaluated by you? What physical characteristics have you chosen to mirror in your body? (You may discover, for example: I have re-created my father's walk, my mother's bad back, my aunt's interest in art, my family's inclination toward poverty, my culture's puritan work ethic, the attitudes toward life taught by my religion which lead to feelings of guilt, the predominant concern in my nation for the value of property and the importance of money, etc., etc.) As you begin to see what things you selected as part of your reality, turn your attention as well to what you did *not* select. (My mother is a worrier, but I'm not; my father was always stingy with money, but I'm very generous; all my siblings have allergies, but I don't; most of my friends are party-goers, but I'm not; my teachers tried their best to discourage me from becoming a doctor, but I became one anyway; I was raised among class-conscious people, but I enjoy mixing with people from all walks of life, etc., etc.) Seeing that you chose some characteristics, but not others, will help you to get in touch with your power to make new choices now. Even if you chose a characteristic early in your life, it can be changed any time you realize that you are the chooser.

Thus you can see that your environment was not determinative, even though it was formative. It provided a shape and form for your early experiences, enabling you to make some initial, albeit unconscious, choices regarding who you would be. As you become more and more conscious of who you are, who you have chosen to be, you can change that reality if you want.

A word about heredity. In order to have a physical body to live in and through on the physical plane, you had to be born of a particular father and mother. There are those who think they, therefore, had nothing to do with their genetic inheritance. Seen from the larger picture, however, you can perhaps recognize that you as a center of consciousness, as a soul, were not born *of* the body, but rather helped give form *to* the body through which you live.

Physical bodies, families, and cultures are rather like learning centers in the school of life. We have to start somewhere, so we start in the particular center we were drawn to as we 'entered' the school for this term. Your drawing to a particular father and mother may have been largely unconscious if you had not yet developed much of an individualized consciousness. In that case, your past learnings and experiences would have determined your attraction to a particular learning center (body and family group), either because it was familiar or because it was very different from any you had ever experienced before, or some combination of those two. On the other hand, if you, in your soul, had developed a certain degree of individualization before this lifetime, you may have consciously chosen your learning center, including your body and parents, for the growth opportunities it offered you.

31

What you were given to work with genetically during this lifetime was yours by choice, whether unconscious or conscious, and is, therefore, a life-time opportunity for your growth in consciousness. Your freedom lies in what you *do* with your genetic inheritance. How you work with, and transform, your given learning center is truly your conscious creative opportunity of this lifetime.

Not only can we not blame anyone else for the reality we chose, then, but neither can we take credit for what anyone under our tutelage (child, student or friend) becomes through our influence. Children, students, friends, employees, or whoever, are the creators of their own realities. We only offer a few of the options that are available to them and they choose which to accept and which to turn down. None of us helps or hinders others. The others take what we offer and help or hinder themselves in our names.

That is why the only sure way to bring any reality into being is to *become* it yourself. If you wait for others to bring it into being, or try to convince or change others, you are dependent on their choices for your reality 'creation.' If you choose to *be the change you want to see happen*, however, no one can stop you, for you are in total charge of your own reality.

Creating Realities Consciously

Finally, it is important to recognize that when you begin to create your own reality *consciously*, you begin, generally speaking, by choosing consciously among the options and alternatives that are familiar to you. As you change your reality, different, new-to-you, options and alternatives will come into your awareness and consciousness, and you will begin to choose from among those as you continue consciously to create your reality. But still, nothing 'new' will have been brought into being by you, nothing original.

Too often persons who learn *about* the power to create, think they can 'create' by an exercise of their own will power. "If I concentrate hard enough on the automobile I want, it will come into being, or if I visualize my husband as completely healed, the effects of his stroke will disappear." Such exercises of individual will or expressions of wishful thinking are not vehicles for the creative power. They may align you, on mental levels, with the creative flow of others, and thus you may indeed get the automobile and/or your husband may indeed recover, but not because *you* brought it into being, but rather because you established a rapport with what was coming into being in some larger framework of reality-creation.

When you truly *create*, your thoughts, feelings and actions are in perfect alignment and your will becomes the vehicle of expression for the larger, or 'higher' will—that will which is expressive of universal harmony, or the natural order process. This is not simply a matter of thinking about it, nor of wanting to, nor of acting in obedience to inner directives. It is a total integration of your being and a bringing of the facets of self into such balance and harmony that the finer energy frequencies of life can move through you unobstructed and you can become a conscious cooperator with the universal pattern of creative unfoldment.

It is only as you begin to open yourself to the Higher Self, the Higher Mind, the divine within, that that which is new, as-yet-unmanifested, will be made known to you in order that you might bring it into being. At that point you become a creator in the true sense of that word. Until then, you are an imitator of the creative process—sometimes consciously, sometimes unconsciously. When you begin to reflect in your conscious mind a larger picture, a wider comprehension, a vision of that segment of the perfect pattern which is waiting to be unfolded in and through you, then you have the joyous privilege of being able consciously to *create*, to bring into form and being what is not yet, but through you will be.

Such creativity is often experienced and expressed first in "bursts"—bursts of creative genius. Some persons bring through one such vision in a lifetime, and spend the rest of their years unfolding it. Others are able to create in certain areas—technology, science, music, art, etc.—but not in other areas of their lives. Only through lifetimes of experience, of practice, in aligning consciousness with the finer energy frequencies do persons become whole in their creative expression. Those persons have been recognized throughout history as enlightened ones, as masters.

You, too, can be a master. You begin where you are with the 'substance' you have been given. Step by step, you will awaken your own creative genius. *First* you become conscious of the reality you have been creating. *Second,* you exercise your choice-making power by consciously choosing between the various alternative realities you see around you. *Then* and only then are you ready to become a conscious *creator* of new realities. The power lies within each of us. The degree to which you consciously exercise that power is yours to choose.

Living In The Energy World

To become conscious of yourself as the creator of your reality is to free yourself to perceive, experience and know the energy world directly and thus to become consciously integrated with it. As you hold in your conscious awareness the *process* by which private worlds are created, you can begin to liberate yourself from the confines of your private world and open yourself to a larger reality. Spiritual awakening comes with that breaking out of the prison of your private world into the vast energy world with which you are one. Learning to create your own reality consciously, therefore, can facilitate your awakening and your eventual realization of your true nature.

The **Love Project** principles are a reality creation. They were an 'original' creation by one of your authors, Arleen Lorrance, who received their simple and direct form in a moment of insight that broke through the boundaries of her private world experience up to that point in her lifetime. The truths the principles embody are eternal and can be found expressed in many other forms and formulas throughout history, but giving expression to the guidance she received from Higher Self, Arleen gave new expression to enduring truths.

The way the two of us have chosen to share the principles is also an original creation in its over-all form, though the elements of our work and life are not new. Our unique contribution has been to find ways to speak with the authority of our personal experience without becoming authorities to other persons, to teach without having students, to strike out on a new course and share that way with others without developing a following, and to develop a Love Family that is ever-expanding without becoming cumbersome, confining or burdensome. We have sought to bring into being a pathway for personal growth and spiritual unfoldment that is as 'new' as this 'new' age.

We hope that these six simple principles will become consciousness tools with which you can build a reality of love in your life in order that you might be of service in the world and live in joy and peace and harmony. We invite you to take them and, with their help, to become conscious of the reality you are creating, to practice making conscious choices about your reality, and finally learn to become a conscious *creator*, bringing new and wondrous expressions of love into being through your own person.

Chapter Three
RECEIVE ALL PEOPLE AS BEAUTIFUL EXACTLY WHERE THEY ARE

This principle is your invitation to step into the univeral flow of life and become a conscious expression of it. It is an invitation to expand beyond the limitations of your own private world—the reality you have created which defines and limits your own experience of life—and to become a channel for, an expression of, the unconditional love which is the unifying force in the cosmos.

There is no way to do this principle if you limit your life experience to your private reality, for within the confines of that inner world of yours, only you can be right, only your approach to living is valid. This principle is not directed at the specifics of life-expression in any evaluative way. It does not have to do with comparing one life expression with another or with judging what is good or right or true and what is not. This principle has to do with experiencing the flow of life in all its magnificence, just as it is, in each given here and now moment.

To put this principle into action in your life, you must open your heart center so that the love which is often called the love of God—that unlimited, unconditional, infinite, life-giving love—can be fully received by you and shared with others.

You will most easily move into the expression of this principle if you will visualize an open shaft of light and love flowing to you in an unending rush of Life, entering at the crown of your head, rushing through your whole energy field, and being released through an ever-expanding funnel of love that opens up at your heart center and expands into infinity, enveloping all as it goes.

Learning to love unconditionally—learning to *receive all people as beautiful exactly where they are*—is learning to move beyond how you *feel* (preferences, likes and dislikes, emotional responses, wants and needs) about someone and what you *think* (judgments, shoulds, oughts, musts, assessments, opinions, values) of them, to the pure experience of being alive and sharing that life with all others. It is learning to love universally as a new mode of loving, rather than learning to love all people the way you now love a certain few.

· Universal love is free-flowing and non-magnetic. It has no strings attached. When you love with heart-center love (open-channel loving in which energy is received and released in a perfect balance) you seek nothing in return for your love. Your love is a response to the love you have already received from the universe. You give it in gratitude, not with the expectation that it will be requited.

Learning to love unconditionally is to learn to live in joy, to be fully alive, to be always grateful under all circumstances, and to receive all persons as special gifts of life/love given to you to quicken and enhance your life.

Perhaps you are thinking, "All of that sounds great. I'd like to be able to love that way, but I find so many people just plain unloveable. How *can* I receive all people as beautiful exactly where they are?"

How To Be Universally Loving

You have already taken the biggest and most important step if you *want* to be more loving and are sincerely asking how. If you want to know the joy, the life-giving joy, of *being* universal love, then there is a how and it is surprisingly easy. Let's take an example which illustrates how you might get trapped in your private world and through unconscious reactions, engage in a most unloving and unsatisfactory interaction, and how, in the same situation, you might move out of your private world into universal love.

You pull into a gas station at the "full service" pumps. It is Saturday morning and you are in a wonderful mood. You are on your way to an outing with friends which you've been planning for several weeks. "Fill it up, and check under the hood, please," you smile at the gentleman who approaches your window. He grumbles something in response as he turns to go to the pump. "Seems unhappy," you note, hardly caring, as you happily let your gaze wander to take in the two young men chatting in the garage door and the woman working behind a desk in the office. You are immersed in your own private world reality, thinking about the day ahead.

The gentleman is passing by your window on his way to the hood of the car. "By the way," you say matter-of-factly, "would you mind checking my tires, too? I'm planning to put some miles on today."

The man does an abrupt half turn and growls, "I sure won't." Then he goes to the hood, opens it, checks the oil, and slams the hood again without so much as a glance at either the radiator or the battery. He's heading back to your window as you're still absorbing his last remark. "I've got a bad back and I wouldn't bend over to check your tires if my life depended on it," he throws at you.

You breathe deeply, thinking, "Wow!" You decide to do it yourself since the guy seems to be having such a hard time. "Never mind," you retort, getting out of your car, "I'll check them myself."

"There's no air pump here," he snaps. You fall back into the driver's seat in response to the sheer force of his words. "Great service!" you're thinking. "First the guy does only the most perfunctory check under the hood. Then he refuses to check my tires. Now he says he's got no air pump." You swallow hard and try once more. "How about the windows?"

"Look," the attendant says, as though responding to a challenge from you. "I've been in business here for forty years and I don't have to break my back for people like you."

You've had it. You snap back, "It's a wonder you've lasted that long!"

His retort is ready. "Nobody can stay in business these days. The big gas companies make it impossible for small businessmen like me to keep our heads above water. It's all a guy can do to stay open."

You're seething by now, feeling put upon and abused. Whatever happened to the old adage, "The customer is always right," you wonder. "I'm surprised," you grumble, "that you have any customers at all," holding out your credit card. "Believe me *I'd* never come in again."

"Thank God," he replies, looking at your card. "I can't take that," he spits out contemptuously, thrusting your card back at you. "It's no good."

"What do you mean it's no good?" you nearly shout, refusing to take it back. "It's a lifetime card!"

"Company issued new cards this year. We're not taking these any more."

By this time the two young men have come closer to hear the debate. The attendant turns to his wife in the office and calls, "What about this?" holding up your lifetime gold card. "No good," she shouts back curtly. "Can't accept it."

"Can't accept it," he repeats to you as though *you* were the unacceptable item (your private world feeling response to his words.)

Your hands are trembling. You'd like to punch the guy, but you can't believe you're into this scene. What happened to your happy mood, your airy Saturday outing attitude? "Just how much do I owe you?" you ask, your voice tight, controlled, as you fumble for some change. You count out the exact $7.12 as you're thinking to yourself, "I should just drive away without paying after the way he has treated me. Why should I put up with this kind of abuse and *pay* for it, yet?"

"But, no," you reflect, "I won't have him on *my* conscience. He's the last person I'd want to be indebted to. I'll just pay and get out of here."

You almost throw the money into his outstretched palm, wishing the coins would fall to the ground. In the same tightly controlled voice—a little louder than necessary—you say," I *do* hope your back is better!" with the most biting sarcasm you can muster. Then you peel out of the station, wondering what you did to deserve such a start to your otherwise perfect day.

The rest of the day is overshadowed by your pent-up resentment at the service station attendant. You are short with your friends, you feel miserable about your own behavior, and you vow never to go into one of his brand stations again! That vow strings out your secret boycott of x-brand gas station for months—even years—and each time you pass one by you think to yourself, "Serves him right." You still seethe inside.

Now, how could anyone love a man like that? He is impossible to receive as beautiful. Or is he?

Let's take a look at what happened to see how you might have loved him. You went into the station focused on *your* day. The attendant was not a person to you, he was a means to an end. He would get you ready for your long-awaited outing. You viewed him only as an instrument. He was there to serve you. That's all. You did not make any room in your life-space for him as a human being. Perhaps that's where things began to go wrong.

To love people is to *receive* them into your energy field and into your consciousness. It is to acknowledge them as the human beings they are and to recognize that your life is quickened by their presence. It is to exchange the gift of life with others consciously. Since you made no room for him, he had to fight his way into your awareness.

You might have started with a simple "Good morning," or "Hello, there," pausing long enough to experience him, to recognize him, to honor him as a person. Then when the quickening of your energy by his began, you would not have been taken off guard. If you had consciously welcomed him into your life-space, you could have *responded* to him instead of reacting.

But supposing you didn't think to do that and the scene had proceeded as before until the gentleman said he wouldn't check your tires and then went on to do an incomplete check under the hood of your car. You might have become conscious then of your own process, your own reality creation. What were you thinking? Were you striking out in criticism in the silence of your inner space, thinking, "this is no way for a gas station attendant to act," or, "I'm not getting my money's worth," or "how dare he treat me like this?" If so, you might have made a choice then to *create a new reality* for yourself in order to *be the change you wanted to see happen.* If you didn't like his speaking to you in such curt tones, you might have begun to *think* kind thoughts about him in preparation for your next interchange. You might have thought, "Obviously something is wrong. He's having a bad day. Maybe I can bring some joy to him."

And you might have observed what was going on with your Little Self, that deep-feeling child within you. Were you beginning to be angry in response to his words and actions? If so, you could have chosen to create a different feeling—one that would be in harmony with your highest and best response, rather than just being a reaction.

You might have breathed deeply during that interim, recalled that you have had bad days yourself and know what that's like, and chosen to send him love and caring through your heart center, by-passing the reactions of your hurt Little Self and your critical mind in order not to add to his distress. When you saw how little he was willing or able to give to you, you might have decided to serve *him* in his moment of need, letting your abundant and joyful life energy flow freely to him, perhaps even openly expressing your concern and caring for him.

He opened the door a little—gruffly, to be sure—when he told you of his injured back. You could have let him into your life space and consciousness then. You might have chosen to feel compassion for him in his pain, instead of choosing anger at his refusal to serve you. You might have explored alternatives with him regarding the healing of his back. You might have told him that you, too, have suffered from a bad back and could understand his not wanting to bend over to check tires.

And when you started to get out of the car to check your own tires, you might have done so in a genuine spirit of helpfulness and consideration, instead of as a challenge to him, as a way of showing him what a lousy service attendant he was. You could have been more thoughtful of him than you felt he was being of you.

If you had really wanted to receive him as beautiful right where he was, you might not have even asked about the windows, but instead have simply cleaned them yourself, feeling you could do that much to help him out. Continuing to function out of your **expectations** that *he* would clean the windows only invited further antagonism in him *and* you.

By the time the issue of the credit card was raised, you were aware that the whole interaction had been reduced to the level of a spat between two school children. Instead of going on with it, you might have just laughed and shared with him how silly you felt for getting so upset with him. You might have thanked him for telling you about the new cards and ***provide him with the opportunity to give to you*** by asking what you should do about your lifetime card, or if he had an application form you could have for one of the new cards.

Any of these alternatives would have been a "how" in that situation, for the how simply lies in opening the energy flow instead of blocking it, and in making way in your life space for the other person *as he is*.

Receiving all people as beautiful exactly where they are, and thus loving them, is a way of keeping the Life Force moving through you so that you remain alive and well and have a life-giving impact on persons around you. It is not just a fancy ideal; it is a practical approach to happy and healthful living. What was accomplished by the interaction as described above? The man in the station was unhappy and hurting before you came in. You certainly didn't relieve his condition by your presence, and more than likely, you added to his distress. Moreover, by reacting to him in kind—being brusque, thoughtless, impatient, resentful, angry and hurting—you altered your own reality, which had been a happy and healthful one, and created unhappiness, frustration, resentment and anger within yourself. You took that away with you. It put a damper on your long-anticipated day with friends. It made you less loving toward them and toward all others you encountered that day—and even toward some people in the days that followed, whenever you were reminded of that attendant and your resentment spilled out inadvertently.

Responding to So-called 'Negative' Energy

To love others by receiving them as beautiful exactly where they are is to love them unconditionally, with no strings attached and no walls or barriers built up to hide behind or keep others out. When you meet someone like that gas station attendant and you feel them to be functioning in 'negative' energy, you might well say to yourself, "I want no part of such a person. *I* am practicing being loving and life-affirming. I do not want my positive feelings and attitudes brought down by this person's negativity."

But in so thinking, you move into the very negativity you want to avoid. A person has just come into your life and you have said 'no' to him. You have chosen to invest your energy in non-receiving. *You* were the one to label the person's energy 'negative,' and therefore the negativity is your reality creation. It may also be the other person's reality, but you have just made it yours, for you saw it, you labeled it, you determined it was something to stay away from.

You might say you have created a **problem** for yourself, for now *you* have to find a way to cope in *your* life with negativity you have taken on by so labeling it in another. You are experiencing negativity even as you say you want no part of it. Now you have to find a way to get rid of this 'negative influence,' as you view it. A struggle is on—one in which you may expend enormous amounts of energy.

Had you made the choice to be totally loving, instead of meeting a person with negative energy you would simply have met a person. Then, like drawing in a deep breath of fresh air, you would have welcomed the person into your life space, experienced the quickening or enlivening effects of being touched by his energy, and then released him at once by letting his energy flow on through you.

Let's take another example. You're out walking your dog. There is a city ordinance that says dogs must be on a leash at all times, but your dog is very well-trained, very obedient, and no threat to anyone, so you let her walk freely alongside you. You see a woman approaching. She is being dragged in your direction by her large dog on a leash. You tell your dog to stay and she does. Then you hear the woman shout, "You'd better watch out or you'll soon have two dogs." You breathe deeply and let the woman and the words she has said come into your life space. You experience her energy as jangled and are confused by her words. You wonder if she thinks her dog is going to try to mount your dog and make her pregnant, thus resulting in the 'two' dogs to whom she refers. You breathe again, letting her jangled energy go, and say, calmly and kindly, out of your own reality, "It's all right; she's been spayed."

It is clear the woman does not hear what you have said, for she goes right on. "That's what's wrong with this world. I feel sorry for your dog. She seems nice enough, but she has a lousy, irresponsible owner, and if you don't put that dog on a leash, I'm going to let my dog go and it will tear yours in half."

You let the energy in, and register astonishment at the vehemence of it. You understand now what she is reacting to, so you breathe her energy out, reach down and take your dog by the collar, turn without a word, and walk the other way. As you go, you breathe your blessings to her, hoping that your actions will not continue to cause her distress. You wish her well on her way, and reflect on your part in the interaction. Is it irresponsible of you not to have your dog on a leash when other dog owners have dogs that cannot be trusted if set free? You make a new choice about walking your dog, vowing always to carry a leash and to put your dog on the leash when other persons or animals are in your vicinity. You thank the woman in your thoughts for having called your attention to your possible negligence before something unfortunate happened because of it.

Here was an instance in which you might have reacted to the woman's 'negative' energy. Instead, you *received her as beautiful right where she was* and consequently did *not* create negativity in your own energy field and did not alter your reality to match what you perceived to be hers. You let her into your life space and responded to her from your own center, choosing to be loving and also choosing to receive whatever message she was bringing *for you*. Having received her energy and let it go, you were free to respond to her words and the thought behind them, rather then reacting to the manner in which she offered them or the feeling tone the words conveyed. You were free to love her because of her apparent distress and anger, because of your part in evoking that distress in her, and because she had done you a favor by calling your attention to the possible consequences of your actions without your having to suffer or to cause others to suffer. You could send her gratitude and blessings and let her go in freedom. You were better off for the interaction, and so were others with whom you have come into contact since then, because you chose to fully receive her in that unique moment in time.

Being able *to receive others as beautiful exactly where they are* requires receiving self as beautiful, too. In the above situation, for instance, if you had passed judgment on yourself in her name, you might well have felt the need to defend yourself against her. She criticized you, and in this case, you agreed with her criticism, at least to a large degree. However, instead of beating yourself up about it, and feeling guilty, you simply made a new choice. You *received yourself as beautiful right where you were* and did not seek to explain to the woman *why* you did not have your dog on a leash.

If you hadn't received yourself as beautiful exactly where you were, you might have felt frightened by her gruffness and/or hurt by her criticism and sought to hurt her in return. By not choosing out of fear, but rather out of astonishment as a feeling response, you didn't feel the need to bring her down to the size to which you would have reduced yourself by saying, "Well, if you can't control your dog, that's *your* problem," or, "If you'd train your dog to obey you it wouldn't be a threat to other dogs it meets in public places." By receiving yourself as beautiful, you could choose a loving response to her, *being the change you wanted to see happen* in that very moment, rather than being pulled down and back by actions and decisions which were already in the past. You had love to give her because you first received love for yourself.

Receiving Includes Letting Go

To receive persons as beautiful exactly where they are is to welcome them into your energy space *and* to let them go in the next moment. In the case of someone who is functioning out of energy that you do not choose for your own, as was the woman with her dog, it is only by releasing her energy that you can choose a different manifestation. But the principle holds equally true in the case of someone you find most appealing and delightful.

Let's say, for instance, that you are at a party. You are introduced to someone new, and you are immediately drawn to him/her. You like the way (s)he looks, the way (s)he speaks, the way (s)he dresses. You find him/her exciting and dynamic. You want to be his/her friend.

In this case you may not wait to welcome this person into your life space when (s)he 'arrives.' Instead, you may rush out to greet him/her, ushering him/her into your life, eager to have him/her be a part of you and you a part of him/her. You not only want him/her to come in, you want to "have and hold" him/her, and never to let him/her go again.

Your eager welcome of this new person into your life can indeed be an expression of universal love. Your desire never to let him/her go again, however, is not. It will surely create energy blocks, for in your attempt to 'keep' this person, you must invest energy in a holding operation, and that energy cannot be available to you for interaction with that person or with others either.

When you receive others as beautiful exactly where they are, and yourself as beautiful, too, you are acknowledging that you are all whole beings. Your energy fields can touch and interact, thus enhancing each other's lives, but one cannot become caught in the other without inhibiting your life flow, thus diminishing your capacity to live and love.

If you truly love persons unconditionally, and also like them a lot and enjoy having them around, you will receive them as beautiful in each new moment, relishing the gift of life they bring to you, and release them in the next moment so that they are absolutely free to offer that gift again and again, to you and to others. To cling to what you first receive is to live in the past, missing the beauty of each new moment as it comes. If you try to hold on to someone you love, you will awaken one day to discover you no longer know him/her, for the person you love is the person who *was,* when you first met. That person has been alive and growing and changing all the while, but because you did not want to release the gift first given, you have not been open to receive the myriad of gifts offered since, and thus have become a stranger to the one you wanted most to know. You will have created the very reality you wished to avoid, for by attempting to hold on, you actually missed the opportunity to continue to receive and to love as the days went by.

Conscious Activation of the Breath-Flow

How can you receive all people as beautiful right where they are? By remembering to breathe in the midst of interactions.

When you pause to breathe, visualize your life space as individual molecules of dancing, swirling energy easily permeated by the molecules of energy of another. When you inhale, expand your own field, making room for the other person's energy, which you are drawing in on a parallel flow. As you exhale, contract your own life space slightly, simultaneously letting the other person's energy pass on through. Physical breathing is a wonderful mirror of the process of receiving another's energy, and the two together, engaged in consciously, will facilitate your loving interactions.

In fact, it is also by breathing that you draw in the Life Force which is the gift to you of love energy from the universe. When you breathe, you fill yourself with life. If you breathe consciously, you can receive the gift of life as a gift of love and experience gratitude for both at one and the same time. If you will begin to be aware of your breathing, you will find that whenever you are having difficulty receiving yourself and/or others as beautiful exactly where you/they are, you will have stopped breathing, or at least reduced your breath-flow to its absolute minimum. You cut off your own life source by refusing to let that love energy flow to self or another. By the simple act of consciously initiating the breath flow again, you will find it much easier to receive both self and others as beautiful. Thus, when you begin to feel "This person is impossible," or to think, "I can't love this person," remind yourself to take a deep breath, give thanks to the Universe for the constant influx of love and life, and as you exhale, begin to share that Life Force with all around you. In sharing, you will have opened the door of your being to the other, and welcoming them in will be much easier.

"Receiving" as Contrasted with "Accepting"

Receiving, then, involves the active taking in of energy and the passive release of that same energy after absorbing it into your own life-space. But to receive is not the same as to accept, to approve of, or to like. It is possible to fully receive persons you disapprove of, dislike and/or would not want to be like. You do not have to *accept* for yourself their manner of expression, their style of life, their values, attitudes or morals, in order to *receive* them. To receive them is simply to *experience them fully in your consciousness just as they are.*

Supposing you have a friend who is talented as an artist and capable as a businessperson. He has had his own business for many years and has done well in it. At fifty, your friend decides to sell his business in order to find his way in a new style of life. He does not take another job. he goes from one place to another, trying out lifestyles that might be right for him. He borrows money to travel several times. Friends help

47

him pay his bills. He finally ends up living with a woman who supports him.

You have always had strong convictions that paying your own way and being a financial success in business are two of the most important values in life. It would be unthinkable for you to, as you would call it, "live off" other people. Moreover, you feel each person should earn enough to put away retirement funds so they do not become dependent on public funds in their later years. Can you receive your friend as beautiful exactly where he is in his new lifestyle?

Yes, if you *want* to. All you have to acknowledge is that *you* would not do what he is doing, but he *is* doing it. Instead of spending your time criticizing him (whether in your thoughts or directly), you might receive your friend as an opportunity for you to get on the inside of another approach to life. By receiving him into your life space, you expose yourself to someone whose approach to living is very different from yours, whose private world reality is a challenge to your own. You may come to understand his way fully by receiving him just as he is and not trying to change him. It is not necessary for *you* to take on his style of life in order to know and understand it. You can continue your own experiment with living, and at the same time expand to include another approach by receiving your friend as beautiful right where he is.

You would not be receiving your friend as beautiful where he is, however, if you tried to rescue him, and therefore it is important that you remember to release his energy after you have taken it in and experienced it. Therefore, if your friend is out of money and wants to travel and tells you of his dilemma, you will want to breathe all that in, experience what he is experiencing, and then let it go. It may be that you do not choose, because of *your* values, to lend him money for travel when he is not working to earn his own way. Then lovingly, freely, tell him you do not want to give him any money. That is your gift to him of *your* lifestyle, and by receiving yourself as beautiful where you are, you will see that if you do not give your friend the full gift of who you are being, you are not truly loving him.

Or, suppose you are working for a woman who is a perfectionist. She arrives early at the shop each morning — before the stipulated hours for work — and begins to do *your*

48

work because you are not there. When you arrive at work *on time*, she tells you what she has accomplished, making you feel as though you should have been there to do it yourself. She takes only five or ten minutes for lunch, and makes comments about how long it seems you have been gone when you return after your hour's lunch break— an hour she has indicated is your allotted time. When you leave to go home at night, she is still there working hard, and often doing over, or adding to, jobs you have spent much time and effort on during the day.

You think she is a fanatic. You have no desire to work that hard or to put your work above everything else in your life. You do your work and do it well and for you that is enough. Can you receive your boss as beautiful exactly where she is?

You can with ease if you will remember to keep receiving yourself as beautiful at the same time. Only if you begin to take your boss' values and attitudes into yourself and apply them to yourself will you feel uncomfortable, guilty, pressured or uneasy in her presence. If, on the other hand, you keep acknowledging that there's where she is because that's where she chooses to be, and that you function differently, then you can simply receive her energy in, experience it, and let it go, leaving room in *your* lifespace for her to be as she is even if she doesn't do the same for you in return.

Or, you are a mother who prides herself on being a 'good' mother to your children. You are home each day when they come home from school. You listen to their stories of what happened during the day. You take them to their piano lessons, to Little League games, to Saturday afternoon matinees. You take time each evening with them before they go to bed. You take care to prepare nutritious meals for them, to keep their clothes in good repair, to keep your home clean and orderly so that your children will have a wholesome atmosphere for their growth.

Next door lives a woman who has children, but takes no time for them. They seem to run wild in the neighborhood. This mother doesn't work, yet she never seems to be home. She is always off playing bridge with her friends, or at her swim and racquet club, or who knows where. In the evenings, she and her husband frequently go out, leaving the children to care for themselves by sitting in front of the TV set. They stay up till all hours, and you have heard they seldom do their homework and sometimes even fall asleep in class. Your daughter tells you that their socks seldom match and their clothes are wrinkled and unkempt because your neighbor never sorts or folds the laundry after doing it. It all stays in a heap in the family room. On weekends, the mother drags the children with her to *her* events, instead of enabling them to take part in activities with children of their own age that would enhance their growth.

Can you receive your neighbor as beautiful right where she is? You can if you will remember that your children are *yours* and hers are *hers*. You raise your children the way you do because of your ideas, ideals, values, background, etc., because of your private world reality. To you your way seems best. Your neighbor apparently does not share your values. She has *created a different reality*. Therefore, she is raising her children the way she is raising them. You can do nothing about that by being critical of your neighbor or worrying about her children. All that would do is to upset you, making you less capable of being a good mother yourself. If you can see some way to *be the change you would like to see happen* in relation to her children — in effect, taking them in and being the mother to them that you would like them to have — then fine. Do it. If not, just breathe deeply, acknowledge that she is certainly a different kind of mother than you are, and let her go. Keep your love energy flowing for the sake of your own family and your own health.

Or, you have a daughter who leaves home at 18 to find her own way. You don't approve. You think she is too young. You are afraid she will get into trouble—drugs, pregnancy, who knows what—and you are sure she will never amount to anything.

If you put a lot of pressure on your daughter to conform to *your* ideas and ideals, you may risk driving her further away from home or breaking her spirit so that she does what *you* want, but loses her zest for life. But if you receive her as beautiful in her plans, then you will be able to share them with her, giving as much input and guidance as you can regarding the choices she is making, and staying in as close contact with her as she will allow in order to hold before her the example of *your* life as an alternative she might choose in her future. If you will receive your daughter as beautiful where she is, you will have more life energy with which to engage with her. You will be able to go on living *your* life fully and still respond to her when she needs you and asks for you. You can receive her because you love her, and if you didn't you wouldn't be concerned.

If you refuse to receive her as beautiful, you will cut her out of your life space and thus disenable yourself from having much influence on her in the long run. You can share how you feel and think and still receive her as beautiful where she is. "I think you're making a big mistake, but it is your life to live and I will be glad to share in it with you in any way that feels good to both of us," you might, in effect, say to her.

Receiving people as beautiful where they are is acknowleging that they are living their lives just as you are living yours—the best way they know how. You might not approve of the way they are living it, but then they might not approve of the way you are living yours, either! That's the reason we each have our own lives to live—so we can do so as each of us pleases and learn whatever we learn in the process.

If you remember that making room in your life for persons whose values and standards and lifestyles are very different from yours does not mean that you have to become like them, then you can begin to experience the joy and wonder of your differences from others, and realize that only by being fully who *you* are and receiving others for who *they* are, can you experience the full potential of richness that life offers.

"Beautiful" Is an Affirmation of Life

That is what "as beautiful" means. When you receive others as beautiful, you do not judge that, according to your standards and values, they are beautiful as contrasted with undesirable. You do not look at what they say and do, at the way they dress and talk and act, and find them pleasing to your taste. Rather, you acknowledge the *inherent beauty* of human beings as expressions of the Universal Life Force. The beauty is in their *being*. To recognize and affirm that being is to acknowledge and affirm life itself. It is to say 'yes' to the Life Force. It is to say, "I welcome Life with open arms and find It/me/you beautiful."

According to the biblical creation story, when God made human beings, He was pleased. He said, "That's very good!" He did not say, "Well, that *seems* to be good, but I'll wait and see how they turn out—how they behave, what they do, whether they make something of themselves, whether they talk to me with respect." No. He gave his unconditional affirmation of this life form He had brought into being. To receive people as beautiful is to make that same affirmation. "Here is another of God's creations and it is *very good!!* I delight in this person *because he is,* not because or in spite of anything he has done or will do. I find him beautiful and rejoice in him."

Most of us do this principle well with small babies. No matter what they look like, we say, "Oh, isn't that a beautiful baby!" We are rejoicing in this new creation just because it has come into being. It does not have to earn our love. We love it just because it is.

You can practice experiencing the wonder and beauty of life *just because it is* if you will use the analogy of nature. How many times have you walked by a dying tree and looked with awe and wonder at its twisted, dry limbs, finding them beautiful? The next time you see an old person, hunched over, bent, wrinkled and brittle with age, look in the same way, with the same eye of wonder. Here is the life process in all its beauty. What amazing and wonderful configurations it takes on.

Or have you watched a sunset with its brilliant hues of red, orange, magenta and rose, and exclaimed with gratitude about the beauty it reveals, not bothering to focus on the fact that it is the pollution in the air that causes the vivid colors to shine forth? Then, watch with wonder the next time you see someone explode in anger. Marvel at the tremendous energy being released, at the astonishing facility with words the person displays, at the *life* being exhibited so dramatically by this being. Never mind that it took anger to set the person loose. Receive the beauty for what it is in that moment.

Or, have you watched the agility of a cat as it makes its way over fences, in and around buildings and cars, up trees and poles, climbing over all obstacles with incredible grace? Then admire the creative agility of a politician when you see him climbing to the top, using incredible ingenuity, dexterity, quick wit, charm, and talent to make his way. Never mind that you might judge him dishonest, two-faced, etc. You are focusing now—without judgment—on his creative use of his life energy. Delight in the beauty of the demonstration.

Be the Change You Want to See Happen in Response

Receiving persons as beautiful is delighting in their being alive, and finding their life process itself something to rejoice in. But just because you receive someone as beautiful, you do not have to be immobilized in relation to them.

For instance, supposing one of your employees embezzles funds from you, and you find out. You can marvel at his cleverness and delight in the skill he demonstrated and *also* fire him, turn him over to the authorities, demand that he pay you back, or whatever action you care to take. You do not have to stop loving him just because he has done you a wrong, or because you are going to take action in response to his deed.

Or, suppose you are a teacher and you find that your students have been cheating on their exams. You can appreciate the spirit of cooperation they demonstrated, the concern and caring they have shown for slower students, their communal spirit and their resourcefulness, while still pointing out to them the rules of the game as you have laid them out in your classes, doling out appropriate punishment, etc.

Receiving persons as beautiful exactly where they are need not render you ineffective or inactive as a change agent. In fact, it will keep your Life Force flowing and enable you to act more effectively with less blocks within you than if you got entangled in emotional upsets and in desires to change the other persons, or critical thoughts about them. It also keeps alive your respect and reverence for the life process itself and keeps you from getting so locked up in your private world of values and preferences that you are not able to rejoice in life for life's own sake.

Perhaps a helpful analogy can be competitive sports. It is possible to engage in a competitive game with the full intention of winning, giving all you have by way of energy to beat your opponent and employing your finest skills and abilities in the process, yet still to appreciate, enjoy, even admire your opponent and the way he is playing the game. Should your opponent win, you can sincerely congratulate him on his victory and wish him well in the future, without in any way intending to give up the game yourself. In fact, you may fully intend to beat him next time you get a chance.

Life is something like that. Very often your moral standards, ideals, and convictions will seem to compete with those held by others. When you look out at society, you may have a feeling sometimes that the "others" are winning. Without giving up what you hold to be the highest and best, and without in any way giving up your energy engagement in the being and doing of your values, you can nevertheless admire the skill and agility of those who differ from you. You can congratulate them and wish them well on *their* life course. You can respect and even admire the intensity with which they are being the highest and best they see and know, and you can rejoice that we are all given opportunity after opportunity to participate, that is, to be alive. Then you can pour your Life Force into ***being the change you want to see happen.***

Supposing, for example, you have spent months of intense involvement in the campaign of a candidate for governor of your state whom you feel can really turn things around in the right direction in the state economy, educational programs, welfare and social services departments, and agricultural policy. You have given your all, both financially and in terms of your time and talents, to see him elected. You *know* he is the best man for the job. Then your candidate is defeated on election day and the person elected is, as you know him, clearly inferior in ability and laissez faire in his policies.

How can you receive the people of your state as beautiful in having elected the 'wrong' person? By recognizing that they, like you, could only vote according to their best judgment. If they did not recognize your candidate as the best, perhaps it is because from where they are in their own growth and experience he was *not* the best. You can be grateful that they voted, thus expressing their own preference actively, and that the person elected will have a clear majority of support so that he can execute his policies and *all* of you can have an opportunity to determine from your own experience whether his ideas work or do not work.

You can receive the voters of your state as beautiful by recognizing that you are only one cell in the body politic, and the wisdom of the whole organism surpasses that of the individual cell. Therefore, what you saw as best for the whole body may not, considering where the rest of the cells are, *be* in fact the best. You can therefore be grateful that the other cells were alive and active enough to make their preferences and will known so that the whole society might stay in harmony and balance and continue to function with minimal discomfort and maximum efficiency.

When you feel you know what is best for another person, or indeed, for the whole society, that *is* what you know. But others may have a different knowing. Only as you each give full expression to what you know can the whole body of which you are a part come to its own state of equilibrium and balance.

Being able to be grateful for the functioning of the whole is facilitated by that joy in the wonder of the life process itself, and the realization that what matters ultimately is not the specific manifestation the Life Force takes, but that the Life Force is being creatively, actively and consciously expressed. The *reality you create for yourself* is only one tiny possibility out of the vast potential of the universe. You cannot express it all, and therefore, you can rejoice that others are expressing their facets so fully and magnificently and creatively.

This Moment Is the Only Time You Have to Be Loving

"Exactly where they are" is the portion of the principle which focuses your awareness on the here and now moment. It is a reminder that whatever you want to do and be and express, the only time you have to do it is here/now. If, for instance, you say you love persons because of the potential you recognize in them, even if the potential is a *divine* potential, you are also acknowledging that you do not love the persons now as they are. You love something you see in them which is not yet manifest, yet what *is* manifest you do not love.

To receive persons as beautiful exactly where they are is to rejoice in their own creative expression, whatever form that is taking, and to delight in what they are. For example, you meet a man and are immediately attracted to him. You fall in love with him. You delight in his company. There are some things about him that you do not like and that bother you—such as his lack of awareness of other persons, his tendency to withdraw

55

into himself for hours at a time and not talk to you or anyone else, his single-minded devotion to his job, his lack of interest in the arts, which you enjoy so much. Nevertheless, you reason to yourself that he can and will change with time and under your influence. "There is so much good in him which is yet to unfold," you tell yourself. Assuring yourself that you *do* receive him as beautiful exactly where he is, and you marry him.

Seven years later, or ten or twenty, you find that he has not changed. You have been raising your children essentially by yourself, he does not take you out to the places you enjoy going, much of your time 'together' is spent alone because he withdraws for such long periods of time, you feel unfulfilled, frustrated, lonely *and* resentful. What are you resentful of? Of the fact that he did not fulfill your *expectations* that he would change. You knew what he was like when you married him and that he was *not* o.k. with you. You did *not* really receive him as beautiful exactly where he was, but still you married him. It is not *his* fault that you are still not receiving him as beautiful where he is. He is just being himself. If you did not love *him*, you should not have married him.

Your problem was that you did not stay in the here and now. You loved some image you had of what he would become at some future time. The future never is. It is constantly being translated, one day at a time, into the present. It is in the *present* that we must live, or we do not live at all.

On the other hand, supposing you meet a woman who is really *it* for you. You find her exciting, stimulating, dynamic, alive, creative, intelligent, expressive. She is a wonderful conversationalist; she is a whole person in her own right; she has a career and is successful in it; she is sensitive to you, shares common interests with you. She makes you feel alive. However, you come from a strict religious background, and this woman is not religious. In fact, she has never belonged to any church, and although she has high moral standards and a deep spiritual sensitivity, she refuses to let you put any labels on that, and she will not go to church. Moreover, she is divorced, which is against your religious beliefs, she is five years older than you, which you *know* will be an affront to your parents and friends in the church, and she has no background of family orientation, having been raised an only child and been left an orphan at 16.

You realize that the two of you share so much that makes for a rich and meaningful relationship. You wonder if you can receive the rest of who she is as beautiful, even though it conflicts with aspects of the ideal you had held for a wife. Then you realize that *she* is the gift being given. Your ideal does not exist—or at least you haven't met that woman yet. Moreover, perhaps those things you see as less than your ideal will turn out to be growth **opportunities** for *you*, ways you will come to expand yourself and your own understanding and expression. With time you come to see that you love *this woman*, just as she is, and that *she* is the one you want to marry.

Ten years later you are aware that in your time together, your wife has come to love family life as you always have. The two of you have found a church to be involved in that is meaningful to both of you and through her influence, you have become more liberal and broadminded with regard to religious matters. You have come to realize that you may have more years to share together because she is older than you are, and not only has her divorce never been an issue or a problem, it has enabled you to be much more receiving of friends who have gone through their own marital difficulties and sometimes divorces, and it has strengthened your own marriage relationship because she learned so much through her first experience about what makes a marriage work. Yet as the years have gone by, your marriage has seemed perfect to you at every point, and you do not feel it is better now than it was when you started, because you have truly received your wife as beautiful exactly where she has been at each given here and now moment.

Receiving Others Enables Them to Grow and Change

Receiving persons as beautiful exactly where they are is sharing with them the full flow of love energy they need in order to be able to receive themselves as beautiful and thus allow their full potential to unfold. You are a teacher. You have been given an entire classroom of senior boys who are repeating Junior English because they failed it last year and are grouped together in your Senior English class because they hate English and tend to be discipline problems in regular classes. "Don't expect much of them or try to do much with them. Just try to get them by," your department head has told you. You determine *not to have any expectations* of them whatsoever, and certainly no negative ones, such as that they will not like English and will do poorly. You decide instead to receive them as beautiful exactly where they are and proceed with *abundant expectancy.*

From the first day you meet the class, you delineate for them exactly what they must do to pass the class, and then you tell them that if they also want to learn something, that would be beautiful. You delight in whatever work they do, praising them for their accomplishments without judging them against some external standard of what they "ought" to be able to do. As the year goes on, they gain confidence in their ability to do well in English. They begin to work harder. Many confess to you that this is the first time they have ever enjoyed English. All but a few are excited and delighted by their progress and are willing to invest more and more of their energy in their work because they begin to see results themselves. They begin to receive themselves as beautiful as English students, and their self-confidence yields ever-expanding results in terms of learning. Discipline problems never arise, not even with those who are spoken of as "incorrigible" by other teachers.

Or, you are a parent. You delight in your children's processes as they are growing. You recognize individual differences between your children and you rejoice in them, receiving each child as beautiful exactly where (s)he is at each stage of his/her growth. You encourage each in the direction he or she chooses to develop interests and abilities. You do not project onto them your own images of their futures, but rather delight in watching them unfold before your very eyes.

All of your children become creative and productive and establish happy and secure homes of their own, though their lifestyles and chosen lines of work and involvement vary a great deal. One by one they return to tell you, as adults, that the greatest gift you gave them while they were growing up was confidence in themselves and in their ability to make their lives count. You know that all you did was love them, receiving them as beautiful exactly where they were at each stage of their growth.

Or, you and your business partner are forced to declare bankruptcy. You face the fact that you just can't make it with things the way they are, but you know that this is not a definitive statement about you as a businessperson. You know that you can and will get through this crisis and find another way to earn your living. There will be other opportunities for you to go into business for yourself and you will welcome them when they come. You receive yourself and your partner as beautiful in your misadventure, expressing gratitude for all you have learned. You know you are a bigger person for having gone through this experience.

Your partner blames you for what happened, feels his whole life is ruined by this filing of bankruptcy. He takes to heavy drinking, and two years later commits suicide.

Because you received yourself as beautiful under very trying circumstances, and your partner, too, you increased the flow of the Life Force through your energy field and you grew and were strengthened by a difficult experience. Your partner, however, refused to receive himself or you or the situation as beautiful, and consequently cut himself off from the Life Force, thus ending his life very quickly.

It is Love that enables persons to grow, as sunshine helps plants grow. By receiving yourself and others as beautiful exactly where you are, you allow yourself to be a channel of the nurturing force of Love in order that all persons might unfold to their full potential starting right here and right now.

There Can Be No Exceptions to Universal Love

That brings us back to small word "all." This principle cannot be done wholly until it is done universally. It is impossible to love unconditionally in relation to one person without expanding to include all, and if you are not loving all persons, you cannot unconditionally love even one.

At first this might seem impossible, or so vague as to be meaningless. However, if you realize that the principle focuses on the here and now moment and has to do with *receiving*, not with passing judgment or feeling good about someone, then you can see that persons come into your life in specific situations, at specific moments, being and doing specific things. They are always individuals, even if they are in groups.

If you focus on receiving each person as beautiful exactly as (s)he is, you will find that you are never confronted with more than one at a time and that the process is really the same with all people as it is with one.

For example, if you try to receive Nazi Germans as beautiful as some amorphous group, you may find it very difficult, for in *retrospect* we can see the impact the *group* has had on history and on other persons. In order to apply this principle in relation to persons who lived in the past, we must receive them as beautiful exactly where they *were*, in their time-space. They did not have the gift of our hindsight, and they were *individuals* acting in the highest and best way they saw to act then and there.

Perhaps you can receive them as beautiful exactly where they were because they were persons selflessly dedicated to a universal cause. They believed what they were doing would make for a better world for all to live in. They believed that their leaders were enlightened. They were willing to forego personal preferences in order to be obedient to a higher authority. They gave themselves totally to the cause they believed in.

Or perhaps you can receive them as beautiful because you realize that had they not been willing to be and do what they did and were, you might not have developed the sensitivities you have today. You might not have realized that we can sometimes become blinded by causes—even the most well-meaning and high-minded of causes. You might not have come to see that any people who choose to set themselves up as judges of other people's fate are bound to commit injustice and often even brutalities against those others. You might not have recognized the danger of blind obedience to authority, no matter how much faith you have in the authority. And so forth. In other words, those persons gave their lives in order that you and others might learn an enormous history lesson in life and living.

Perhaps you can receive them as beautiful when you realize that they could only do what they saw to do as their highest and best expression in that time-space, for that's all any of us can do. For all you know, you are presently participating in some group expression that will have consequences which, in the long run, even you will not approve of. Yet you can only do what you see to do here/now. What is learned from that in the future is part of the contribution you are making by living your life. perhaps you can give thanks for the contribution to our world learning the Nazis have made.

To receive *all* people as beautiful, then, is to recognize that all people are individual persons living out their lives as best they see to live them in their time-space. It is also to receive each individual person we meet in order that, by receiving each one, we become more and more capable of receiving all others.

Perhaps, for instance, you find it impossible—because of your upbringing, your religious beliefs, your attitudes of reverence toward life, etc.—to receive as beautiful exactly where they are persons who kill others and/or take their own lives. Because you do not believe in killing, you cannot, you feel, receive killers as beautiful exactly where they are. Obviously then, you are having trouble moving into the universal expression of this principle.

Then comes the day when your own son shoots his wife, sets their house on fire, and then kills himself beside her. You are stricken with remorse and grief, you feel your heart will break, and yet you *know* all that led up to that day and those events. You know of his terminal cancer, you know that his wife had been seeing other men and that the two of them had been agonizing together over the disintegration of their marriage. You know your son's life had reached a point of desperation. You had tried to help and could not. He had finally exploded, taking his wife with him.

You do not approve, and you wish it had never happened, yet somehow you do understand. You can see how your son could have done what he did, and you forgive him, horrendous as the acts seem on the surface.

Suddenly you find yourself wondering about others who kill or commit suicide. Could it be that they, too, have undergone such suffering and torture that they see no other way? Could their life-circumstances be such that they perceive no alternatives? Could they even see their acts as liberating, rather than destructive? Most of all, you realize that you are not in a position to judge, for you *have* no way of knowing what is going on inside of them. Therefore, through the experience of receiving your son as beautiful right where *he* was, you become

61

able to receive all other killers, and all those who commit suicide, as beautiful, suspending judgment and choosing instead to share with them the Life Force that flows through you in order that both you and they might learn from their experiences and grow in your understanding of the Life Process.

Universal Love Includes Yourself

If you reserve the right to hold onto some condition or reservation in your loving of any one person, then that condition will restrict your flow of love to all. On the other hand, each time you are able to receive one more person as beautiful exactly where (s)he is, you will be that much more able to express your love universally, for when the barriers to love fall for one person, they fall for all.

That being true, there is one simple way to become totally loving of all persons. That is to totally love yourself. If you let go of all judgments of yourself and simply open yourself to the fullness and plentitude of the Life Force that is given to you each day *unconditionally*, then you will discover that you *are* love. You will *know* that you are love and that it is of your nature to be totally loving of all others. You will find that the most natural, the easiest thing to do is to love—to love yourself as a perfect expression of the universal Life Force right here/now, to love all others who live, no matter in what form they are expressing that life, and to love life itself and living itself with a vigor and enthusiasm you have not known before. You will find that you are in joy, as well as in love, and that you are able to give praise and thanksgiving for every gift of life that comes to you in each here/now moment.

Receiving yourself as beautiful exactly where you are does not lead to complacency or smugness. When you truly love yourself unconditionally you recognize that you are essential to the Universe. If you were not being what you are, the Universe would not be what it is. At the same time you recognize that you are no *more* important than any other human being, because all others are absolutely essential, too. When you love yourself unconditionally, you rejoice in your inherent worth as a human being and in your inherent equality with all others. You joy in the the miracle of being alive, asking no more than that and receiving gratefully whatever is added to that basic gift by way of opportunity to experience and to grow. You affirm divine purpose and wisdom, knowing that all is right in the world—even pain, suffering, or what you might label 'evil.'

When you receive yourself as beautiful exactly where you are, you are able to let the full force of your being come into expression, holding nothing back and thus fully developing the potential you have to be the creative Life Force of the universe in manifestation. When you consciously receive the universal Life Force as a gift of love, it moves through you as a dynamic impetus to express your own creativity in universal love and service.

Chapter Four
BE THE CHANGE YOU WANT TO SEE HAPPEN, INSTEAD OF TRYING TO CHANGE EVERYBODY ELSE

In *receiving another as beautiful exactly where (s)he is,* you are, in effect, saying: "I find no fault in you; I affirm your choices and your unique life expression." You may *also* be saying: "I would not make those same choices. In fact, I feel so strongly about *not* doing what you are doing, that I am stirred to make some kind of counter statement or to take some balancing action." In this statement is evidenced the life process itself: polarities mingling in irritation and unrest, inviting the new to come into being.

When you are irritated, outraged, annoyed or angry, you are at an important crossroad. If you seek to change the one you blame for your inner disturbance, you open yourself to energy-consuming complication. But if you decide instead to *become* the change you want to see happen, you move beyond entangling yourself in another's expression and into the creation of the new form out of the old irritant.

Being the change you want to see happen, instead of trying to change anyone else, is moving beyond receiving another as beautiful where (s)he is and where you choose not to be, to being in yourself what you wish the other would be.

Let's look at the example of your neighbor who fights with his wife, yells at his children, fumes at his dog, and makes life miserable for you when the energy of his outbursts reaches from his house to yours. You have breathed deeply and *received him as beautiful exactly where he is,* yet you wish he would change his behavior, or move, or become more civilized, or set a better example for his children and yours.

If you were to invest your energy in trying to change him, you might try a number of tactics—both direct and indirect—like telling him his blood pressure would be lower if he'd learn to cool it, or shouting out your window when he begins to shout and telling him to pipe down, or pointing out that he is destroying himself and his family, or calling the police.

Yet, no one changes another; each of us changes our own self—when we are ready and willing.

If your neighbor were indeed to take your advice and change, it would be because your neighbor made the *choice* to change and not because *you* changed him. By the same token, if your neighbor did *not* change as a result of all your efforts, that would bear no direct reflection on you either. It is not your prerogative to cause change in another's life because you are not the one who is living it. Instead, it is for you to live your own life and to *be the change you want to see happen* through the personality vehicle that was given to you for your own unique expression.

There are many ways you might *be that change* in your own life: you might consciously look at how you are relating to your own mate to see if you are even slightly raising your voice above what is necessary when you are seeking to communicate your point of view. You could be even more loving with your own children, even more tolerant of your own pet. You could even be more gentle with your neighbor and more flowing in your energy with him, thus mirroring for him a different way of relating to other persons.

In *being the change you want to see happen,* it is imperative that you *have no expectations* that just because you are being that change, the one you would like to influence will get the message and make the same change himself. If you are really *being* the change, you are being it *for yourself* and not in order to effect change in another. You are *receiving the the other as beautiful* and using the stimulant of behavior that displeases you to bring about growth in yourself, seizing the *opportunity in a problem.*

The change you seek to bring about is a change in the *expression* of the Life Force, not in the Life Force itself. The Life Force *is.* Its unfolding changes in expression, like the constant shifting of sands, is the process of becoming. We are all engaged in that process. Though we seek sometimes to have others shift their expressions to match the stage of the process we are manifesting, our efforts are futile unless we strike a chord of harmony with the change that is simultaneously going on in them.

A Process of Becoming

The nature of our existence on this plane of consciousness in which we have our life and being is that of becoming. Becoming is the process by which we live, grow, learn, stumble and fall, rise up again in glorious exulation. Becoming is our conscious assessment of who we were, applied to who we are, so that we might glimpse the vision of who we will be. Becoming is a constant perfection: it has no final state of arrival; rather, it is ongoing. Respecting the process of becoming in another as much as we respect our own, enables us to *receive the other as beautiful* and to *be the change ourselves* instead of struggling with the other's choice of expression.

If you have ever had an important goal, one which was all-encompassing, and you have achieved that goal (the final completion of schooling, losing or gaining weight, finding the right mate, healing a condition of dis-ease in yourself, completing a creative project, ridding yourself of a habit like nail biting or smoking, etc.) you will know that the sweetness of the moment of victory lasts a very short time, especially when compared to the investment of energy that was necessary to bring that moment into being. When the goal has been reached, you have arrived not at the end, but rather at a new beginning. Any change you think you want to see is not the be-all and end-all. It is only the step you take to get from here to there, where still more change awaits you.

To have completed school is but the impetus to put the knowledge into practice or to reap the benefits of the degree which has been bestowed upon you. To have arrived at a harmonious weight now involves maintenance. When you have found the right mate, you need to begin to pay attention to how both of you are changing and growing in order that you do not pass each other by, having outgrown what brought you together. To have healed yourself of a specific condition brings you to an examination of how you are living in body, mind, spirit and emotions, in inner and outer environment, in diet, in thought and in deed, all in order not to bring a new condition of dis-ease into manifestation. To have completed a creative project is to have elevated your creative capacity and prepared you for embarking on an even greater project which never would have seemed possible to you prior to the conceiving and executing of the first. Having rid yourself of a habit and tasted the fruits of breaking through a patterned response to life, you will find yourself almost immediatley identifying at least one other such pattern and the desire to move beyond it will be greatly activated by your recently exhibited strength in bringing change into being.

In each case, the supposed end result becomes instead a new beginning which has been showered with the light of your accomplishment and hence has been brought into your awareness.

The wonder, then, is not so much in the *completion* of the goal but in the process of reaching it; not in the achievement, but rather in the achiev*ing.* To say, "I have become," is merely to invite congratulations *and* the question, "What's next?" or "What more do you seek?" Life is a process of becoming. Rather than seeking to change others, you can rejoice in their process of becoming and in the particular state they have reached in that becoming which may be quite different from your own.

This process of becoming is very recognizable in its various stages. It often begins with irritation, especially irritation evoked in you by another's life expression. Irritation is one of the greatest blessings in evidence on our planet. It is the evidence that life is active here. In biology the irritation of one cell by another causes movement between the two and often results in the coming into being of a third. The same process is true in our daily lives. "A" is irritated by "B's" actions or position. There is disagreement in order that a new harmony might be discovered. A compromise greater than either position or action is brought into being by the two antagonists, who actually become *protagonists*, or leading characters (leaders), in initiating the new in this life drama. It is when the two antagonists make room for each other by *being the change* themselves that the conflict becomes a single situation in which both are protagonists or molders of a new reality that is harmonious to both. If one or the other is too rigid to allow the other to claim his/her equal right to participate, the conflict or irritation continues.

Several examples would be helpful at this point.

You are a parent and your child, the antagonist, keeps his/her room in a mess. You are not pleased. You are irritated. Or, you are a wife whose husband has been engaging in extramarital affairs causing you great consternation. Or, you are a teacher with a student who constantly disrupts the class. Or, your parents refuse to treat you as the maturing person you see yourself to be, one who has the right to greater freedom. Or, your boss is inflexible and you need this job even though it is ulcer-producing. Or, you are up in arms over personally intolerable conditions in the world—suffering, starvation, warfare, pollution, waste, animal slaughter, pesticides, you name it. Or, a politician's views and actions leave you wanting to scream.

The "or's" are unending, and rightly so. Life is a series of irritations to new growth and understanding. The more charged up you get by another or a particular position, the greater the use of your own creativity in action will be *and* the greater the clarification of your own position. You have cause not only to *receive another as beautiful* in his seemingly alien expression, but to delight in being inspired to the new by this other so different from you.

What you *do* after you are stirred is the crux of what we are discussing; in other words, how do you choose to *be the change you want to see happen?* Once you have identified the cause of the irritation, it is time to get on with what *you* can do about it. Here is where we separate the *antagonists* from the *protagonists*. Here is where it is important to tackle the principle: *be the change you want to see happen, instead of trying to change everyone else. Be* the change; *become* what you want to have come into being.

From Antagonist to Protagonist

This crucial juncture is where many persons get stuck or lost or frustrated. They do not become the change; rather, they invest their energy in trying to change their antagonist. By not *becoming* the *protagonist*, by *not* bringing the new into being, they merely add to the irritation, bring more of it into being and have *more* to blame on the other. The energy invested simply worsens the situation and does little or nothing to initiate harmony in which both polarities might be brought into equality of recognition and therefore into distinct but equal balance—into a united oneness in which individual uniqueness is honored and brought to stand beside the other.

Parents whose children have messy rooms perpetuate the conflict when "after having tried everything" to get the children to do what *they* want, they lash out by putting their foot down and saying, "This is *my* house; you'll do what *I* want." Though the room might indeed be cleaned, the antagonists remain. The accomplishment remains overshadowed by an unsatisfactory means of achieving the desired result. The conflict will no doubt show up again in some other area of the relationship because the underlying irritation still exists. In this case the actual irritation went beyond what was identified as a messy room to a blatant difference in lifestyles between parents and children. Neither saw virtue in the other's approach. Each continued to advocate his own. By trying to change each other, nothing was changed save the room which emerged clean as a result of dictatorial force.

In order to *be the change yourself,* it is important to ask yourself what you really want. Do you want your child's room clean? If so, it is easy for you to be *that* change: simply clean it yourself.

But the chances are that what you want goes beyond that. You may, for instance, want your child *to clean* the room—that is, to do the work. Will (s)he then be doing *your* work (for which, for example, you will give an exchange—perhaps money, perhaps doing a favor for him/her) or his/her *own*? This is a crucial question, because if (s)he is doing his/her *own* work, then it is not really for you to determine how (s)he will do it.

Or perhaps what you want is for your child to *want* to have a clean room. Since what (s)he *wants* is his/her own **reality creation,** you have no control over that, except by your example. Again, it is for you to *be the change* by making cleanliness so attractive in the rest of the child's environment that (s)he begins to *want* his/her room to be clean, too.

Or perhaps what you want is to teach the child to be responsible. Again, if (s)he becomes responsible, that will be his/her own *reality creation.* Therefore, you can encourage responsibility, reward it, and be a model of it, but you cannot *force* your child to be responsible. That is his/her choice. How you will be the change, then, depends largely on what changes you actually want. Focus on that first. Then move into action.

Often, when we want another to change attitudes or behavior, we are not so much objecting to the behavior as we are clearly indicating our own inability to deal with it. If your husband or your wife is engaging in extramarital activities, you might say to your mate, "How dare you?" or, "How can you?" or, "Why are you doing this?" or even, "Get out!" But under all these comments is, "I am deeply hurt. I cannot handle this. I am in pain. I don't know what to do." This last, "I don't know what to do," is what most often results in perpetuating the antagonism. If you don't know what to do (how to initiate the new, how to move the stuck energy, how to *be the change you want to see happen,* how to get on with becoming the more that you are), you focus your attention on trying to change the *other* in order that you might feel better. To try to get the other *to stop* is *not* to do anything. It does not bring any new energy into being. To stop is to attempt to deaden, to kill off. To stop goes nowhere. It is important that if you are the one who is irritated you realize that the other person's action is *not* what is causing the irritation in you. *You* are creating irritation in yourself as a response to the other's action as *you* define that action. Further, you are creating irritation in yourself in relation *to* yourself and your non-action, your non-effectiveness.

In terms of *problems being opportunities,* you, as the heretofore injured party, might wish to *create a new reality* for yourself by, for example, being honored by your mate's action rather than belittled by it. After all, the fact that your mate is attractive to others is an affirmation of your choice and that your mate chooses to remain with you as his/her primary relationship even in the midst of other interactions is a salute to you. This example is not offered as an excusing of behavior that you have labeled intolerable, but rather as a way for you to at least affirm yourself while you go about assessing what it is you want to do. *Being the change* comes best from a base of wholeness and strength. It is from weakness that one attempts to change another...because the attempt to change another arises out of not knowing what to do yourself.

In this case you might be the change by focusing on what there is to affirm in you and rejoicing in it; by being so enriched by your own interaction with yourself that you are not dependent on others for their praise of you; by evaluating *your* needs and involvement in your marriage as it is and seeing whether it is still valid for you to continue in it; by devoting your energies to making your mate feel so loved that he/she won't want to go elsewhere; by openly exploring with your mate your own reality about your marriage and *providing him/her with the opportunity to give to you* by sharing his/her reality with you—his/her feelings, needs, dissatisfactions, desires, longings, hopes, appreciations, joys, fears.

What is important is that you act out of your own creative center as an expression of yourself, not as a plea for help from your mate or as an attempt to manipulate his/her behavior. You can take him/her into consideration by *providing opportunities for him/her to give to you,* to share realities with you. You can express your own feelings and thoughts openly in order that he/she be aware of your responses to his/her actions. But if you have *expectations* as to what response you will get, you will limit yourself and your mate and perhaps stifle a learning/growing *opportunity* because you view it as a problem. And if you are not able to *receive him/her as beautiful exactly where (s)he is,* (s)he may feel trapped, cornered, caught, and fight his/her way out of the relationship just to find breathing space, room to be who (s)he is.

Receiving your mate anu yourself as beautiful exactly where you are, even when you seem far apart, gives both of you the space you need to evaluate your marriage and your individual growth patterns and then to *make choices* that will enhance both of you as each of you does what you need to do to *create a new reality consciously* and *be the change you want to see happen* individually and as a couple.

Focusing on Process

As we proceed with these examples it is important to note that in *being the change* we are not involved in finding final solutions (of which there never are any) but in becoming conscious of the process involved in moving energy and in identifying the change you want to become in relation to what you are wanting to bring into being.

As a teacher in a classroom situation where a disruptive student is making it incredibly difficult for you to get on with presenting material as you have planned to present it, you are facing the universal situation of will pitted against will. It is similar to the home situation in that the authority figure (teacher or parent) defines the mutual space (classroom or home) as belonging to the one in charge and not the underling (student or child.) The disruptive student does not fit into the framework as outlined by the authority figure and "must be made to conform." There is even an appropriate justification which is that it is imperative to learn appropriate behavior in order to function in society. From the point of view of the so-called disruptive student, (s)he may be feeling his/her way toward coming to know how far (s)he can go, what his/her limits really are, how assertive (s)he can be and still survive. Student and teacher in this case may represent the direct antithesis and therefore perfect harmony in relation to each other.

In trying to still the student, you as teacher actually engage in the exact behavior you see the student exhibiting. You attempt to exert your will, to make your point prevail, to overshadow if not out-shout the disrupter. You know that you are right and that you must win if you are to be able to go on teaching in the way you have determined is harmonious. The student, your perfect mirror reflection, may be exerting his/her will to make his/her point prevail. (S)he feels (s)he must be allowed to express him/herself, and not within prescribed bounds, in order for enough flow of energy to be present to be able to learn. If (s)he is forced to be bottled up in his/her energy expression (s)he has no avenue open for the new, including what you have to offer as a teacher, to enter in. You are so perfectly at odds, so incredibly strong as antagonists, that given the slightest opening you move beyond your point of contention to allowing your individual potential to flow and to making room for each other as protagonists who together might evolve an entirely new educational process in your classroom.

72

You might *be the change* by viewing the student's behavior as interjection rather than interruption, as vigorous expression rather than outburst. This immediately opens the way for a flow of energy rather than the throwing up of a wall of resistance. In resistance comes antagonism. In flow comes the possiblity of harmony.

You might create room in yourself for spontaneous behavior expression, either at assigned times or in those moments when it comes up. This immediately incorporates the 'outbursts' into the whole instead of leaving it out there as an isolated challenge. You might simply go to the student and embrace him/her as a way of receiving the student's energy and giving some as well.

You might take time to get to know this student outside of class—to find out what (s)he has to share that is putting him/her under so much pressure that (s)he bursts out in class, unable to contain the inner reality, yet not finding an outlet for it either.

You might want to open a channel for unstructured self-expression in your classroom as a way of *providing all your students with the opportunity to share* of their inner *realities* with you and as a way of breaking out of patterns of *expectations* and of learning to respond to and interact with your students out of *abundant expectancy, receiving them and yourself as beautiful exactly where you are* in any given moment.

Moving Through as a Way of Changing

As long as one of you persists in demanding that the other change, stuck energy rules. A way to move past a point of stagnation is to move through it and beyond it, taking with you what is of value in it. This is a more detailed process and yet an easier one in that it acknowledges the worth of the other's position while equally acknowledging your own.

A case in point would be you as a child who wishes to be treated as more of an adult by your parents. Your parents, out of concern for you, fill their responsibilities (legal and parental) by laying down the law about the type of persons who are acceptable for you to have as friends, about smoking, drinking, and other moral issues, about the keeping of proper hours, etc.

You, as the child, or shall we say the maturing young person, are ready for, eager for, greater freedom. In presenting your case, you might say, "Trust me," or, "Give me the freedom to prove to you that I *can* do what you want." A seesaw of energy creeks to and fro between the two as the one wants to ride faster yet is worried and the other wants to set the pace but doesn't have the authority. The parents are saying, "be more responsible," and you are responding, "give me more responsibility," and yet neither is willing to totally trust the other. You wish they would see your point of view, and they wish you would see theirs.

You as a maturing young person have a clear opportunity here to move *through* the stagnation by actively affirming your parents' position as a way of **being the change you want to see happen,** by taking the time and energy to walk in their shoes for a time. If your parents say, "We want you in by midnight because (1) it's not safe for you to be out later, (2) we can't sleep until you get home, (3) you need your sleep," etc., you, rather than arguing or trying to convince them otherwise, or continually asking why or complaining, can actively affirm their concern, can make it a love gift to be on time so that they can feel secure (rather than doing the same act as if it were a restriction), can affirm the importance of looking out for healthfulness by getting proper sleep. This is the step of moving *through* the parental position rather than fighting to by-pass it or eliminate it. It is to fully taste of your parents' concern and viewpoint. It is to affirm them in it by being grateful that they care enough to institute it and to want to enforce it.

Having done this step, and done it fully, you are now in a far better position to say, "I want or need more leeway because (1) parties last longer, (2) my dates and I like more time together, (3) I can take care of myself because you have taught me to have concern for my safety because of your concern for my safety, (4) I do have plenty of sleep as witnessed by how well I look after myself on school nights, (5) I *can* sleep later on the weekend. I would appreciate your consideration of my needs as I have considered and still do consider yours, and I hope that you can see your way clear to allowing me greater freedom."

This mature statement can be made by one of any age when that one has indeed gone *through* the other person's position and acknowledged the validity of it while still affirming self-goals. Having walked in another's shoes one can more properly fit into the next larger size one desires.

Going *through* a point of stagnation and affirming the other person's perspective does not necessarily mean that the other person is going to change over and let you do what you want. When **being the change you want to see happen**, you may be the only one to change. The one you had hoped to change may still be proceeding in the same old way. If you have **expectations,** if you do what you do *in order* to bring about desired results in another, you may be gravely disappointed. Going *through* another's point of view enables you to enrich your own, but not necessarily to change another's. The other is enriched only if he chooses to come through yours as well. By being willing to go *through,* you gain even if you do not effect change in the basic situation. Change has happened in you. Because *you* are different, nothing is the same.

Expanding your Creativity

As regards not effecting change in the basic situation, it is important to realize that there is always more than one way to **be the change you want to see happen.**

Let's look at a situation in which your boss is so inflexible that you know you are creating ulcers in response, and yet you don't see any alternatives open to you because you need the good income you are earning and you know that comparable jobs are hard to come by.

Perhaps in your attempt to **be the change** you have worked doubly hard on each of your assignments and presented simultaneously what your boss asked for and what you felt to be a creative alternative. True to his non-flexibility, he chose the former and you were left holding the creative bag and your mounting frustration. This then is the moment to go forward with yet another way to **be the change you want to see happen** rather than to go throw up your hands and resign yourself to hopelessness.

You might, for example, decide to submit your creative alternatives to other companies doing similar work. Since you already have a job, you will not be under pressure to impress anyone and can proceed with **no expectations but abundant** *expectancy.* A new opportunity might just open up to you.

Or, you might share your ideas with fellow employees as a jumping-off place for creative exploration, not in order to build a case against your boss. Exploring with your peers in *abundant expectancy,* you never know what newness might emerge.

Or, you might *be the change* by preparing *three* attempts at the same project—your boss' version, your version, and a third which would be a combination of the two. *Have no expectations* when you make your presentations or you may provide yourself with more fuel for frustration. It might be that it would take years of this kind of double and triple processing for your boss to be ready to receive something other than what he envisioned. In the meantime, you will have not only fulfilled your job requirements and satisfied your boss, but you will have been fully creative besides, letting your productive juices flow rather than eat away at your stomach.

Another way in which you might ease your ulcer creation is by actually being what you are wanting your boss to be—more flexible. Hence, you might want to practice being as open to him as you wish him to be to you and you could begin that process by seeing that you may actually be inflexible toward what you are terming *his* inflexibility. By investing your energy in affirming his choices rather than pushing your own, you might indeed create an environment in which so much praise flows that your concepts receive it as well.

Or, you might *be the change you want to see happen* by practicing total flexibility and maleability on the job, learning as much as you possibly can from your boss from doing things his way, while building your own empire of creativity in your leisure time. Starting a pet project which you alone direct, manage and guide will give you an outlet for your knowing and convictions and may even become a viable alternative to your present job.

If you don't succeed at first, there may be a good reason!

Dealing with 'Overwhelming' Problems

Effectively *being the change you want to see happen* involves a honing process in which you conscientiously reduce a situation to its smallest component parts and begin by dealing with the smallest parts rather than attempting to tackle so large an area that you end up defeated before you begin. In this regard, world situations which seem insurmountable are wonderful practice sessions in honing.

If you find starvation among the world populace a personally intolerable condition, you know that there is nothing you can do as an individual to feed every person across the globe who is suffering in this way. Your conscience does not allow you to say, "Oh, well," and turn your back on it all—yet, you don't know what to do. You now have the opportunity to bring this major issue down to the level of your own lifestyle and to your own home, knowing that each family's choices multiply to create world conditions. There you may indeed find immediate steps to take as your contribution toward alleviating the suffering which is so abhorrent to you.

Examples of how you might *be the change* in what seem like small ways and yet are major avenues when multiplied by thousands of others also seeking to add their efforts are: cutting down on unnecessary consumption; contributing money to causes which directly supply food to those in need; eliminating meat eating so that grain now fed to cattle may be more equally distributed throughout the world; sending love energy on thought or prayer waves to those who are suffering; alerting friends and relatives to ways in which you are helping in case they too might want to add their efforts to yours; urging your state and federal representatives to pass legislation which will help eliminate the causes of hunger throughout the world; inquiring about conditions in your local community where you might make a direct contribution of money, food, time and energy to help feed the hungry; studying to learn more about world hunger so you can more effectively help eliminate it.

The more ways you come up with, the more ways you *will* come up with. Once the energy of *being the change* is set in motion it snowballs and possibilities are inexhaustible.

If there is a politician whose antics send you up the wall, it is well to bear in mind that people who stand for the antithesis of how you are choosing to live, represent an incredible gift to you. By doing what they are doing as their unique expression of the human family, they free you up to be and do what you see as harmonious. You do not need to fulfill their roles in the larger scheme of things because *they are*—and they are doing what they are doing fully. Remember, too, that you, in your contrary life expression, may be driving your adversary up the wall. Neither of you is right or wrong. Neither represents the one and only way. Each of you simply represents one way and it is all the one ways that truly represent the whole.

Pushing your way through force, evangelism, coercion, cajoling, salesmanship, etc., is an exercise in futility in that even if you were to indoctrinate the entire population of the world to your way, you would *still* be expressing only one way in many. The strength of any position cannot be determined by a body count of its rank of supporters. The number of hamburgers sold by a chain in a certain number of years, the number of converts to a particular religion, the amount of votes accumulated by a candidate—none of these tabulations in any way indicates that the brand of burger or religion or political platform is better than others, but only that it has gained a a certain popularity.

To fully *be the change you want to see happen* in relation to the politician who irritates you, then, is to *receive him/her as beautiful where (s)he is* so that you have all your creative energies free for your own activities. Whatever energy you invest in resenting him/her, in resisting his/her approach to life, in criticizing him/her and trying to discredit him/her is energy you *give* to him/her and his/her cause. A negative energy investment is nonetheless an investment.

If you *receive him/her as beautiful where (s)he is,* however, you have all your energies free to invest in being and doing what you want to see happen to counterbalance what the politician represents. For example, perhaps you feel a certain politician is against growth in your local community. Instead of trying to silence his voice, you could *be the change you want to see happen* by initiating and promoting growth in the areas you feel would be helpful to the life of the community. Or, if you feel a given politician ignores the problems of minority groups, you could start a support program which is designed to help minority groups to identify and deal with their problems. Or, if you feel a politician gives too much attention to certain private interests, you could organize or join and support groups lobbying for public interests in the areas that concern you.

The point is to be aware that what *irritates* you in another is designed to *activate* your own creativity. What you see as *wrong* in another is calling your attention to what is *right* for you. What you would like to *stop* outside you points to what you can *start* from within. The world around you, and everyone in it, is given to you as a mirror in which to see yourself more clearly. Whatever you notice 'out there' is an indication of something you can give more attention to 'in' you. If you set out to change the person or circumstance that disturbs your status quo, you may miss the gift being offered; a clearer perception of the contribution *you* can offer to the world. Whatever you *see*, you have the potential to *be*.

Moving on to the More

Being the change you want to see happen can also begin with a stimulus that delights, as differentiated from one which irritates, you. If you are deeply in love with someone and you are wanting an even fuller and more profound expression of that love, you have the opportunity to build on what you already have going for you. If you are constantly inspired and moved by your religious affiliation you may want to seek ways to be even more active and participatory. If you enjoy giving things to others in need and you wish more people would do it as well, you might want to *be* even more of the *change you want to see happen* by giving even more of yourself and sharing the joy you find in giving with others, perhaps inspiring them to do the same.

To be sparked from a base of joy into yet greater joy is as much a part of the process of becoming as shifting from dissatisfaction to improvement.

More often than not, contentment seems to be a condition in which many persons prefer to rest. They arrive at a plateau— at what might be called a veil of consciousness—and they stop there in their pleasure, perhaps hoping to preserve it, and do not part the veil to see what, if anything, lies beyond. Beyond dissatisfaction there is contentment, beyond contentment joy, beyond joy bliss, beyond bliss—yet another veil. As there is no end to our becoming, so there is no end to what we may become, nor any end to the dimensions of consciousness which await us.

The nature of life is becoming. Every life situation is our opportunity to become more of who we are in our vast potential. Step one is to catch a glimpse of the more that is possible. Step two is to clearly determine what we see as conceivable obstacles. Step three is to find as many ways as we can to act on what we see as possibilities.

In beginning this process, it is necessary to move from what you don't want to what you *do* want. In order to *be* any change, you need to know what actual changes you might like to be. Instead of focusing on what is lacking, what is wrong, what is unsatisfactory in a given situation, focus on what could be added by you, what you could do to bring more harmony, what you might initiate to make a scene more satisfactory. By zeroing in on what you want, you can more clearly see what specifically you can do.

If you are in a market and you are seeking a particular non-sweetened product and you find that all that is available to you is a wide variety of sugar-filled versions or artificially (chemically) sweetened versions, you are being presented by life with an opportunity to be an active agent for change. You can, of course, give in, give up, or simply go elsewhere. The moment is there for you and it is up to you to decide what you will do with it. Let us say you decide to seize the moment, to say there is here/now a possibility to bring change into being. Now you ask the all important question: What can I do? What do I want to do? To facilitate bringing change into being, state what you would like to see happen in a concise and positive statement. For example, "I want to make a non-sweetened version of this product available in this market." This is your objective. Notice you have not said, "I want them to stop selling this other junk." (A negative approach and a stopper.) Nor have you said,"I want them to make this available for me," (which would be to try to change them rather than sparking you to find ways to bring it into being.)

Having stated an objective which feels feasible to you, examine what the possible obstacles might be. You do this to expose what you might be harboring as ways to sabotage your own objective. Some examples in this case might be: (A) I have no say at this market. (B) There probably aren't sufficient shoppers to warrant stocking it. (C) Nobody really cares about good health. (D) I'm not a manufacturer. Now it is important to examine your obstacles, as you have defined them, to determine their actual validity or power.

(A) You have said you have no influence in this market. In truth, though you are not hired to do the ordering, it is because you (and all the other customers) shop here that this market is here at all. If not for you (and the others) this branch would be out of business. Therefore, perhaps you have more influence than you think.

(B) You don't know how many shoppers would delight in having the added choice you want to bring into being. You've never asked. For all you know, many have glimpsed the vision just as you did, and let it fall. So many, in point of possible fact, that the vision, brought into configuration by a multitude before you, waits here in the energy environment to be acted upon, and this is how you glimpsed it in the first place. If you *really* want to know if there would be others who would buy unsweetened products, you could conduct your own survey of shoppers here.

(C) To say nobody really cares is the ultimate cop-out. It is the way individuals excuse their own lack of initiative and responsibility. A big "They" with a capital "T" is invented and all the ills of the world are blamed on Them or on some invisible, actually non-existent, It, capital "I." When you say nobody cares you are really saying "I don't care. Or, at least I don't care enough to investigate enacting a change." 'No-body' is equivalent to 'no single person' and you are one such 'body.'

(D) It is true you are not a manufacturer, but is that a deterrent? The real question is, does anyone manufacture unsweetened canned goods? If you investigate, you will find the answer is 'yes.' Even though you are not a manufacturer, you (and the market) do have access to the products you want to see in the store.

Now you have swept your lurking obstacles out of the closet known as handy deterrence and have seen them for what they are. The first was false and limited labeling of yourself by yourself. The second involved a pessimistic leap into the future based on no tangible evidence. The third was a blow by a gloved fist with no person or substance behind it. The fourth was a misleading statement of truth, which turns out to be irrelevant.

When you come to know your obstacles or enemies intimately, you no longer need to have fear of them. Fear is evoked in relation to the unknown, and you have made them known.

Now you are ready to move into action. You know what you want; you've exposed what you thought lay in your way. Now you will move into the how of bringing what you want to see happen into being. You accomplish this by selecting active verbs to propel you into activity. Some samples in this particular case might be:

1. To inform
   a. to obtain information on the pros and cons of sugar intake
   b. to distribute the information in front of the market
   c. to bring sugarless samples to the manager
2. To enlist support
   a. to distribute petitions
   b. to organize a letter campaign to management
3. *To provide others with the opportunity to give to you*
   a. simply to ask the manager to stock sugarless products
   b. to write major companies requesting that they augment their line
   c. to write manufacturers of sugarless products and ask them to send salesmen to your market

4. To shop exclusively in health food stores

Having selected your activities, you move into action, of course with **no expectations** but only with **abundant expectancy.** Once involved, a continuous flood of new possibilities will come to you if you stay open. Frustration has no room to fester where participation flourishes.

The wonder and joy of catching a vision and following through on it is that vision-catching is almost epidemic in its nature. The more you do it, the more visions of new possibilities present themselves to you in all areas of life.

In this regard, **being the change you want to see happen** is a way of activating in yourself the power of creation. It is a way of coming to know the God-Force in action intimately.

Each of us *is* the Life Force being Itself and becoming more of who It is. In order to become more of who we are, we must first *be* who we *already* are. To the degree that any one of us is not actively being all that we can be, the whole is diminished by its ill-functioning part.

To be or not to be is a statement that deals appropriately with life and death. To be less than you are able is to die more than you live. To be who you are, doing what you are able to do, is to shift the balance to life—healthier life, more creative life, longer life.

No matter what the situation, if you are aware enough to see a better way, it *is* possible to bring that way into being. It *is* possible for *you* to bring it into being. And you do not need more than the one you are to set the change in motion once you decide to *be* it. When you *become* the change, it *is!*—whether or not anyone else recognizes it, responds to it or joins you in it.

What seems difficult in one moment is almost taken for granted in the next when the inconceivable becomes reality because one person became it or achieved it. You can **create a new reality** for your life any time you are willing simply to **be the change.**

Chapter Five
PROBLEMS ARE OPPORTUNITIES

To **be the change you want to see happen** is a special challenge when you are confronted with a person or circumstance that you experience as problematic. The temptation in such situations is to try to, or wish you could, change the other persons involved or return to your former status quo. To get in touch with what change you want to *be* in light of the circumstances you are in requires an examination of your own values, talents and potentials.

A problem is an opportunity. A problem stops you or interferes with your life in some way. The opportunity may be to let go of the former way of living and start anew. A problem irritates, annoys, bothers you. The opportunity is that you are being stimulated out of complacency, stirred to new possibilities, nudged into the awareness of how you have been living. A problem is like a stone wall that is dropped into the midst of your life journey. It seems to block your way, to be a detour, to be impassable. The opportunity is to reassess, to regroup, to leave excess baggage behind you, so that you may cross with ease into the new that only appears to be inaccessible from your current vantage point.

Problems range from minor to serious to terminal. Minor problems are small irritants. You start out on the road and discover you've left your shopping list (documents, toothbrush, alarm clock, plane tickets, etc.) at home. You express yourself appropriately: "Nuts!" "Ugh!" "Oh, no!" You need to make quick decisions about how to remedy the situation. The expression of exasperation thrusts you into action and you begin to move the energy that appears stuck in your focus on what's missing and needed by you. Once the energy begins to move, the problem *becomes* an opportunity. The problem was *not* that you forgot the specific item. The problem was that you were distressed or disturbed that you forgot it. The opportunity was not to go back and get it or to find some way to proceed without it. The opportunity was to release the energy you were holding in tension, in anxiety, in self-punishment, in annoyance. The problem was minor in terms of the relatively small amount of life energy held by you and the rapidity with which you were able to set it moving again.

Monitoring Minor Problems

Minor problems have a way of aggregating and becoming major in their impact in the long run. Therefore, each minor problem offers you an opportunity to become conscious of how you interact with those daily run-of-the-mill occurrences in life. Do you flow with them, receive them, delight in them, or do you tense up, regret, rebel, reject them?

If you tend to tighten rather than flow, it is because you are experiencing the events as problems rather than opportunities. You are saying, "No" and thus *creating* problems for yourself, rather than saying, "Yes," in which case you would create opportunities. Mind you, there were neither problems nor opportunities to begin with. There were only you and your life circumstances. Then *you created your own reality* in relation to those circumstances. If you doubt this, simply remind yourself that there is always more than one way of looking at anything. You don't even need another person around to have a second view. All you need is a new attitude toward the circumstance, a different point of view, a different frame of reference, and magically, a situation that seemed terrible or had the potential to be terrible, is easy, or "no problem," or "just one of those things."

To become conscious of how you handle minor-life-circumstances and whether or not you choose to create problems or opportunities of them, observe your behavior in the midst of each event.

You go to the post office and there is a long line. *How* do you wait? Patiently, idly, in appreciation that you will eventually be served, in great annoyance, fidgeting, chatting with others, feeling critical of the system and how few clerks there are working, purposefully, creating time pressure for yourself, being totally present to the here-and-now moment of your life, thinking only of getting out, being grateful that you are alive and able to stand there? Note how *many* possibilities there are. You were given the circumstance, as well as the free *choice* as to how to respond to it.

In the moment that you observe in the midst of such a circumstance that *you* are creating a problem, *you* can make a new *choice, create a new reality.* You can open yourself to the opportunity.

A major difference between a problem and an opportunity is that in the former, the energy is bound; in the latter the energy flows freely. When energy is bound, reverberations are experienced throughout the life systems of the one *creating the reality* and of those around that person. If you are blocking energy, you are producing pockets of tension and soreness in your body which can rapidly become places where dis-ease festers. In your mind you may be producing cutting, destructive, inharmonious thoughts. The feelings you choose may be heavy, thick, painful. From all these areas, sparks fly off your energy-body as if from a faulty match being struck again and again without success. These sparks of dis-harmony dart in and out of other persons' energy fields and may stir interactions of ill-will between you and them— interactions which you may then use as yet another indication of the "problem."

This can be clearly seen in the post office example. You've been waiting in what *you've* decided is an interminable line (actually for about five minutes). You've been pondering the inefficiency of the postal system and feeling cheated of your personal time. You've not been breathing very deeply. You'd like to tell them a thing or two, but you feel nothing would change anyway. Finally, feeling as if you've been held prisoner and tortured, you approach the counter. You are not smiling. What has just 'happened' to you is in no way funny. The clerk smiles and says, "May I help you?" You think to yourself, "Trying to make up to me, eh? They trained you to smile at me, but it doesn't make me feel any better. I won't give you the satisfaction of receiving that smile. I will not allow it to appease me when a grave injustice has just been done me. Yes, you can help me. You had *better* help me and you'd better be quick about it!" Gruffly, but not too overbearingly lest the clerk respond in kind, you thrust your package forward and say only "First Class." Your sparks are flying. They reach the clerk who has no idea what's going on with you and rather than get involved, chooses to retreat. When the transaction is complete, neither of you is very satisfied.

At this point, your minor problem is a candidate for what might be symbolically called your 'preserve shelf.' The situation has been prepared, waxed over, lidded, and stored in a small compartment of yourself. You didn't really move the energy. You are unfinished with the incident, but you are choosing not to deal with it or take responsibility for it. Later in the day, you may take this 'post office jar' off the 'preserve shelf' and tell a sympathetic friend how "They did it to me at the post office." No doubt the listener will commiserate with you. You will feel like a victor. Yet, nothing will be resolved. You still see the post office line as a problem. You still think the same thoughts about it. You still feel the same way. The energy you call up in relation to that scene is fixed, held, awaiting your re-creation.

To move the energy is to transport self into the opportunity that the problem represents. The process begins at any point along the way—at any point you wish to initate the conversion. You may begin years after the event by remembering back and saying, "I certainly invested a lot of my energy in creating distress over having to wait in post office lines." You may begin the day after the event by making a new choice about how to relate to post office lines and then actually going to the post office and practicing your new approach. You may begin in the midst of the actual event by asking yourself, "Hey! What am I doing? It's ridiculous to get tense (create tension) over this." You might simply want to say to the clerk, "I know it's not your fault but I certainly don't do well waiting in lines like this." Such a statement moves the energy and allows the configuration of the event to be dispersed rather than preserved. You might begin the moment you walk into the post office and observe the line. You could say to yourself, "There is a line. This will take a while. How do I want to occupy myself while waiting?" Or, "Do I want to come back later?"

Whether you have problems or opportunities is wholly up to you.

Moving from Creating Problems to
Seeing Opportunities

Minor problems have brief duration. You stub your toe; the pain soon goes away. A slow poke on the highway is eventually passed by you. A part that breaks is easily repaired. Minor problems are given limited energy involvement on your part.

When you stub your toe you might shout or mumble under your breath at what got in your way or at your stupidity for not watching where you were going. Your opportunity may be to awaken your consciousness to your relationship with physical objects surrounding you, or to focus on moving in harmony with your capacity, and not *over*-extending yourself. To thank your toe and the object for meeting is to open yourself to what you are telling yourself as differentiated from complaining about what you have done to yourself.

The slow poke driver is an irritant to you because he is in your way, he is not handling his vehicle in the way you think he should, or you feel he is doing this *because* he wants to aggravate you (even though he doesn't know you at all.) Here is an opportunity for you to *be the change you want to see happen,* and whether or not you pass him is not the real issue. You feel the driver ahead of you is in your way. Could it be that your *feelings* about the driver are what are actually blocking you, disenabling you from moving ahead in a free flow of energy? You can let go of your feelings, get out of your own way, breathe deeply, relax, and wait for an opening on the road ahead that will match the openness in your own energy flow.

You want the driver ahead to be considerate of you. Are you being considerate of him? Perhaps he is afraid to drive more rapidly on this road. Can you be compassionate? Perhaps he doesn't know the territory. Have you never driven on a strange road? And what about the drivers behind you? Are you as focused on being considerate of them as you wish the one ahead were of you? Perhaps you want to expand your view of yourself on the highway, and instead of focusing solely on the car ahead of you, see yourself in the larger picture of the traffic flow. Then you might make new choices as to how you can facilitate that flow, maneuver your car in relation to the many, rather than concentrating solely on the one you see as blocking you.

Did it ever occur to you that whatever the driver ahead is doing has to do with him and not with you, and that if you see him as doing it *to* you, you are abandoning your own centeredness of being and *allowing* your vehicle to be blocked by his? Your opportunity may be to see that he is simply driving at *his* rate of speed, as are you. Therefore, he is *not* a slow poke, for there is really no greater virtue in the way you drive than in the way he drives. Your opportunity may be to see that the life-force is expressed differently by each of us who lives it and that unless you acknowledge and respect the uniqueness of the driver ahead of you, yours is not being honored either. You may want to see what you can learn from the driver—open yourself to the gift he represents and experience gratitude for him, rather than creating irritation in relation to him.

If a mechanical part breaks and causes you inconvenience, the energy you invest in creating a problem of the event is the energy you invest in delaying the repair. When something breaks down it may be your opportunity to have a first-hand affirmation of the temporalness of life in manifestation on this plane of consciousness. To acknowledge that is to hold ever present in your awareness, gratitude for what does work, when it works. When something breaks down you can build up the quality in your personality self of taking nothing for granted. It may be an opportunity to become more respectful, and less dependent on outer conveniences.

Problem or opportunity: it's a matter of *how* you see it, *what* you want to see, *where* you want to invest your energy.

Serious Problems Point to Major Opportunities

Major problems are "serious." They have a deep, altering, prolonged effect on your life. They cause extended interference in your life—not just for a day or a week, but over a considerable time span. Major problems take on an identity of their own due to the energy invested in dealing with them. They become like the uninvited guest who adds insult to injury by refusing to leave. A major problem is more than a stumbling block; it is a road block. You cannot pass through it until you are fully cleared and approved.

If you are stricken with an ongoing illness, you have a major problem. So, too, if you are in the throes of a difficult relationship; if you are financially insolvent; if you're pregnant without wanting to be; if you are a perpetual failure at something; if you are in a job which offers you no creative satisfaction; if you are handicapped in some way.

It is important to realize that coping with major problems, dealing with them, learning to live with them, is not necessarily a virtue. For major problems, rather than *being* the disharmony, are really only the manifested *symptoms* of disharmony. If you become proficient at coping with the symptom, expert at keeping it under control, successful at managing to go on in the face of it, you might completely by-pass the opportunity that awaits you. What you are calling the problem is what you have brought to the surface in order that you might see what opportunities lie in the inner pool of your being—opportunities which are causing waves of discontent which have thrown up this splash presenting itself in the guise of a problem. If you are dealing only with the splash and drying out the unsightly puddle it has brought into your life, you can be sure there will be more of them in the future. When you don't get the point, you give yourself the same substance to deal with again and again. Here are some examples of how this works.

Going Beneath the Surface

You are ready for a shift in consciousness, let us say, to a plane where you can actively experience your oneness with all of life rather than experiencing your separateness or isolatedness. To prepare you for the shift, the inner pool begins to send ripples across its surface. Your body cooperates by slowing down. *You* are being asked to slow down. A change of lifestyle is in order. You are being asked (by your own inner voice) to expend less energy. It takes a great deal of effort to perceive and experience yourself as separate from the world around you and from other persons; it would take far less to know consciously your oneness with all there is, for you would no longer have to struggle, or fight, to maintain your sense of ego.

You have not brought this data up to the surface of your consciousness. What you feel at the present moment is more tired more often than usual. So you decide to continue in your present lifestyle. You begin to push your body, to make demands on it. You tell it it can't slow down because of all the things you need to do. One morning you awaken with the flu. You can't imagine how you "caught the bug." You have the supposed problem treated with penicillin and as little bed rest as you can get away with, and you're off and running again. The use of the word "running" is highly appropriate in this case. By dealing with what *appears* to be the problem and not reaching in to discover the source of it, you are indeed running away from the opportunity. The more you engage in this process, the greater the distance you put between yourself and your opportunity, and the deeper you have to journey inward to retrieve the insight that awaits you down the long corridor of your inner self.

You trudge onward in your rugged individualism, arming yourself to cope with whatever might splash in your way and seek to stymie you. For weeks, you take vitamins in abundance; you make sure to get sleep; you exercise. Then the flu strikes again. Now you are really annoyed. What's the matter with you anyway? How could you have a relapse after all your precautionary efforts? But you have yet to ask what the opportunity is, and your inner voice will not be dissuaded. It continues to send you messages. If you don't get it in one way it will come in another. Your evolutionary development will not be permanently delayed by your willfulness.

Several months go by. As if from nowhere, you are stricken with heart disease. You are flabbergasted. How could it have happened? Now you are really down. You can't fight *this* problem; it's too big, and you haven't the physical energy. Your doctor is called to rescue you. M.D.s (Manifestation Doctors) are summoned to correct, repair, heal the result you have brought into being. They deal with seeable, touchable, testable, operable, treatable form. That is their business. They do not, they cannot, cure *you;* that is, they cannot enter your inner pool of wisdom and plug up the opportunity that bubbles there. That opportunity is unformed energy speaking to you in a voice that only yo 1 can hear—that is, when you are ready and willing to hear it. You move from "your will being done" to "Thy will be done" when you shift from willfulness to willingness.

91

The doctor deals with the manifested form of disharmony that you have brought to the surface. If you do not dive deep into the fathoms and depths of your being, you do little to participate in the real healing which has to do with what brought this result into being.

If you are weak enough, if you were stopped profoundly enough, then you *have* to listen because you have been given (you have given yourself) a major problem and you can no longer go on as before.

Major problems, then, are loud crashes on the calm beach of your being. They are rough seas which demand that you navigate with concentration.

Now, as you lie in your bed unable to proceed with life as usual, *now* you go inward. You ask: "What am I trying to tell myself? What is the message of this illness? What is my opportunity?" You have opened yourself. You are vulnerable. You are ready. You can hear your inner voice telling you of the shift in consciousness. You are ready to bring it into being. Now you must choose between the old and the new, between one lifestyle and another.

If you say "no" to the opportunity, you open a pandora's box of ongoing problems because the opportunity will not be contained.

If you say "yes" and cooperate in every way possible to facilitate the coming into being of the new, you will discover how incredibly fluid your life can be. How, even when riding rough seas, you are fully in charge of navigating your vessel to safe port.

When confronted with any so-called major problem, meet the splash by diving into the heart of it and submerging yourself in the life beneath the surface which holds great promise for you.

Throughout it all, be good to yourself. Be kind, be gentle with you. Major problems are not easy. They are not meant to be; else, how would you hear their message? *Receive yourself as beautiful exactly where you are* in the midst of the turmoil. In this way you encourage yourself to go on, and to go deeper in.

Taking a New Look

Briefly, let's look into some other examples of major problems to see what possible oppportunities might be lying in wait beneath the surface.

If you are having difficulties in a relationship, one of your opportunities may be to change yourself rather than demanding that the other person change to meet your assessment of how things should be. How do you feel about such a statement? Does it get your dander up? (Are you using it as an excuse to get your dander up?) Does it strengthen your convictions that you know that you *are* right and that the other person does indeed have to be the one to change? In either case, whether you reject or accept the possible opportunity being presented to you by this problem, stop whatever you are doing to look at the intensity of energy you have invested here and how much blockage there is of that energy. Energy that is not flowing configurates in a problem; when the way is opened by you, the opportunities surface. Initiate the flow by: sharing your feelings with the other person, by asking questions about how the other perceives what's going on between the two of you, by *wanting* to move beyond the deadlock.

Perhaps your opportunity is to move on from this relationship. It may have served its purpose.

Perhaps, while the two of you continue to engage with each other, it is time for a whole new form of relationship to come into being—one which will be newly compatible with your new selves.

In your love of one another in the midst of your problem, your mutual opportunity will come clear. Love *is* unblocked energy. Unblocked energy reveals opportunities.

Financial problems may be symbolic signs of faulty expenditure of energy, or misappropriated energy. You might be seeking to take in more than you are giving out and are therefore creating imbalance. *Im*balance is the outer representation calling attention to the inner opportunity to bring *new* balance into being. The water image holds true here again in that it is often said as regards financial matters, "You'll just have to sink or swim." If you invest energy in dealing only with the problem-apparent (by taking out loans, borrowing from friends, seeking handouts, declaring bankruptcy) you may sink *even* if you survive the current crisis. The sinking, suffocating as it may seem while you go under, brings you below the surface for the deeper look you need.

Most problems are ways of saying there is more for you to look at, more for you to know, more for you to do. Major problems are the undertow that drags you, in your reluctance, from safe but troubled ground into the vast ocean of possibilities that call to you like the roar of pounding waves in the still of the night.

Unwanted pregnancy is about as blatant a symbolic representation of the problem/opportunity process as can be described. The inner self may be so potent with new potential and so open to waiting possibilities that it moves on its own, refusing to wait any longer for action on the part of the personality. It gives the potential the lifeform it needs lest it be aborted. This symbolism can be as true for the man involved as for the woman who is actually bearing the "unwanted" child. If a man is stifling his creativity, holding back his burgeoning potential, settling for less then he is capable of being, he may "inadvertently" produce a replica of that confined energy in an *off*-spring, unwanted though it may be.

Looking at major problems symbolically is a way of telling self about the opportunities that seek birthing through you. By asking, "What can this possibly mean?" you open the way to a flood of pictures which, when pieced together by you into a composite that is perfectly balanced, will be the unrestricted view you were seeking. When proceeding with symbols it is important to **have no expectations** of what you will find. Proceed with **abundant expectancy** by being alert to all the clues.

If you are a perpetual failure in life (in school, in relationships, in your work, in sports, in popularity, in any one aspect of life that is important to you) one of your first opportunities may be to refrain from beating up on yourself and thus adding to the failure. If you flunk out of school and then forever label yourself as stupid, you are forever failing by continually reliving that one failure. There are persons who by all accounts are incredibly successful, self-made persons who because they flunked out of school have never enjoyed their accomplishments as much as those who admire them have.

In any experience of failure, the opportunity may be to focus your attention on what you *are* able to do, rather than on what you aren't. The failure itself may be presented to you in order that you abandon a path you have chosen which is not right for you. Staying with the example of school, if as a child you didn't do well (in penmanship, in math, in grammar, etc.), rather than viewing this as your first failure you might have been encouraged to explore this as your first clue that you were otherwise inclined. Contrary to standardized beliefs and societal regimentation, knowledge of biology is not necessary for a musician, mastering history will not make or break an athlete, educational degrees do not necessarily produce innovators, and medical training may or may not be essential for healing!

It takes some people a long time to get the message. Some even need to flunk out of graduate school to see that the academic approach is not *their* approach.

Failure in any one way is your opportunity to ask, "What is my way?"

Lack of creative thrust in the work you do day after day may clearly be a mirror of the stagnation building up in your inner pool of resources and opportunities. The process involved in problem/opportunity exploration is "as above, so below." By looking into the one that is being shown to you, you open yourself to the hidden implication. When you are willing to move in one area (in this case, perhaps, away from the current job no matter how secure it is) you are ready to uncover the new that awaits you.

As for being handicapped in some way, here again you are otherwise-able. Perhaps your opportunity is to see yourself in your own unique wholeness rather than comparing yourself to others and rating yourself the lesser.

In any major problem, your opportunity is to go within rather than comparing yourself with others or "solving it" the way others prescribe.

Learning to Welcome the New

There is a commonly accepted assumption that life problems have a solution. This is a major fallacy. Math

95

problems have solutions; life problems do not. Math problems are ends in themselves, existing for their own sake. Life problems are facilitative symptoms urging you to go on to the more.

Your problem is something that cannot be solved. "Fix it" in its present form and it will re-enter the stage of your life wearing a new costume. Your problem is a gift to be unwrapped and looked into. It is more what is inside and less what is outside that is demanding your attention. Your problem is a door to walk through in order to discover the new. If you "solve" the problem, you may lock yourself into the old.

Terminal problems are ends offering totally new beginnings. Hence, the opportunity in a *terminal* problem lies in acknowledging that it is *transitional*: a death of the old and a birth of the next that awaits delivery into manifestation.

Terminal problems come in many guises: physical death, being fired from a job, having your house burn down, divorce, death of a mate, etc. Each represents a definite and clearcut end, and each opens the way for the next to enter. Physical death is the temporary shedding of one body for the possible putting forth of another (dependent upon whether or not it is in harmony for you to incarnate again.) Being fired is a traumatic end to creative expression in one form which sets you free to find another. The burning down of your home and possessions is an opportunity to begin again, surrounding self with a new identity. Divorce or death of a mate heralds the completion of a phase of the uniting process currently in progress in your inner masculine/feminine nature.

Because a terminal problem is an ending, it is often frightening and unwanted. Though you may be all too sure of the ending it represents, you may not be at all sure that there will be a new beginning, or *what* it will be. From the vantage point of the ending, it is difficult to find solace in the knowledge that the greater the problem is, the greater also is the opportunity.

To move to the opportunity, to the transition, you must be willing to leave the ending...to let it end. If a mate has died or divorced, let go. Go on with *your* process if you need to, but let the other go. If your home is gone, turn from the ashes and do not dwell on what used to be. If your job is lost, do not linger in "if only." If your body is dying do not cling to it in your consciousness.

Get on with the new by centering your awareness in the present moment, letting what was, and is no more, fall away.

Your problem is of such great magnitude *because* you are capable of dealing with it. We are never given (we never give ourselves) more than we can handle at any given time. To *think* or *feel* that you are not capable is correct in that it is not your objective mind or feeling self that *is* capable. To *know* that you are capable is to activate your untapped potential by functioning through your intuitive or Higher Self in which reigns all the wisdom you will ever need to carry you through the seeming vacuum of this ending into the as yet unformed energy of the new beginning.

Let go totally in order to receive the new abundance totally. The more you hold on to what is dead, the less room do you make in yourself for the new to form.

Don't get stuck in the inactivity of asking *why* did this happen. Rather, begin with the question, "What?" "What can I do now?" Moving the energy in action, in doing, is leaving terminal behind and revving up the rebirthing qualities of transition.

Your mate is gone. What can you do now? Begin by saying "Who am I?" Not, who *were* you when you and your mate were one unit and part of your identity was derived from your union, but who are you *now*—as a whole person in your own right.

Your job is ended. What do you want to do now? The same kind of work? Something new? Assess your skills. How would *you* most delight in re-employing them? Who will you honor by making those skills available?

Your home is destroyed. What is the first new gift you would like to give yourself? Having to begin again affords you a wealth of possibilities. Where? With what colors? What environment? What objects are in harmony for you *now*, as you begin anew.

Your body is dying. What can you do about it? You can prepare yourself for whatever comes—a miracle, a healing, a moving on. You can take this time to finish, to clean your life slate, to forgive self and others if that is indicated, to express any feelings that have been imprisoned. You can open the way to the new by making new choices and beginning right now to live as the new being you would like to give birth to.

A terminal problem is a chance—a chance to change, in the greatest sense of the word. The change comes with or without you, with your permission or without it. If that change is a tragedy, it is because you make it so. If it is a transition, it is because of your willingness to know it as that. What you do with what you are given, determines what next you will be given.

Learning to Live in Joy

A problem, be it minor, major or terminal/transitional, is a problem only if you say it is. By saying "no" to what is offered to you, you attempt to build a barrier between you and it. You struggle to keep out what is already in. To acknowledge that it is indeed already in, and to creatively probe the myriad ways to activate, stimulate, and utilize the energy, is to open yourself to the opportunity.

There are choices to be made in relation to problems. Whether or not you see any opportunity is purely a choice on your part. You might say, "How can I possibly see this illness as an opportunity?"—as if it were insane to view it that way. Another might say to you with equal amazement, "How can you *not* see this as an opportunity?"—as if it were insane not to view it that way. The latter is saying, "You can't afford not to look for the opportunity because if you harp on the problem you may never get well." The former is dwelling in self-pity, wanting to evoke sympathy, hoping to get to the help of others because of the energy invested in the problem.

To say "yes" and to move to the opportunity is to face up to what *is* and to do something about it. To say "no" is to ignore what is in the hope that it will go away simply because you don't want it. To say "yes" does not eliminate your privilege to have preferences. You can prefer to be in a state of harmony. You can prefer to eliminate difficulties, to have only simple challenges with which to deal, to have nothing interfere with your status quo. Having preferences is your prerogative—as long as you are careful to acknowledge that your preferences may or may not eventuate.

Beyond preferences, which are individual interactions with life, there is what can best be termed Isness, that which is, whether we prefer it or not. What *is* comes into being at the impetus of the whole, the Plan, the Larger Good, the Overview,

98

whatever you want to call it. What *is* is the result of more factors than any individual can control or even be aware of. The individual response to what *is* is in the form of preferences: you like it or you don't. But that doesn't change what is. Preferences are merely what you feel or think about what is. What you *do* about what *is* is the determining factor in whether or not what is becomes a problem or an opportunity for you.

A problem is an opportunity to praise life in whatever form it is given to you. It is an opportunity to move beyond preferences to embracing the beauty, the gift, in every single aspect of life—especially those you don't want or like. To be thankful, truly thankful, and deeply grateful for *every*thing is to create a state of being in which there are never any problems because no energy is blocked. No life situation is turned from and shunned. All are welcomed as stimulants, as challenges, as practice sessions in being and doing the highest and best you know to be and do. No congestion is created. Instead, energy flows; joy abounds even in sorrow; and awe replaces fear; love supercedes resentment.

A problem affords you the privilege of acknowledging the opportunity in every seeming crisis. Rush into that problem with your arms wide open and life will hug you in return.*

---

*For a gentle, sensitive and carefully developed process of moving from problems to opportunities with the guidance of your own Higher Self, read Arleen Lorrance's *"Why Me? How to Heal What's Hurting You"*, Rawson Associates, 1978.

Chapter Six
PROVIDE OTHERS WITH THE OPPORTUNITY TO GIVE

We often create problems for ourselves in relation to other persons because we feel uncomfortable with their differences. If they have chosen to hold values different from our own, to wear clothes we would never wear ourselves, to behave in ways we find offensive, to hold opinions and points of view opposed to our own, or to relate to us in ways we would not choose or prefer, we are tempted to withdraw from them, to avoid them, to cut ourselves off from them, to deny them access to our beings. We experience them as problems because we refuse to receive the gifts they come bearing—gifts born out of their differences.

Each person is an individual, and therefore each has a unique contribution to make to life. Human beings are like snowflakes. No two are ever exactly alike. Even persons called 'identical' twins know they are distinct persons and are clearly identified as separate beings by those who know them. In order for the entire body of humanity to be whole, each one of us is essential. What we contribute cannot be duplicated by any other.

If persons do not give of themselves, if they do not make their unique contribution to the whole, it is generally because they have not found, or felt, opportunities that fit the gifts they have to offer. Each of us looks for, even longs for, the opportunity to make a gift of ourselves to others. We want to feel useful, needed, wanted. We want meaning for our lives, and we sense that meaning comes from what we give of ourselves to others. "There must be a work for me to do"—a "vocation," as it is called in Christian circles; a "dharma," in the Eastern tradition; "something to do with my life, some reason for living," as almost anyone would describe it who has felt the debilitation and ennui of a sense of aimlessness, uselessness, unwantedness.

One of the greatest needs a human being has is to be needed. Our sense of self-worth comes almost entirely from the feelings that (1) we have something to give, (2) we can give it, and (3) it is recognized and appreciated by others. Therefore, if we want to be loving, if we want to give to others, one of the most effective things we can do is *provide others with opportunities to give* to us. When we do so, they cease being problems to us and become resources instead.

For those raised in the Christian tradition this principle may at first seem contradictory to the adage, "It is more blessed to give than to receive." However, when we realize that the word "blessed" means "happy" or "fortunate," then we can see that the one who gives is the fortunate one, for the joy of giving is his. If we insist on always being the *giver*, we deny those to whom we give that greater happiness that would come from giving to us. If we *provide them with opportunities to give* to us, we, in fact, love them more. We recognize their worth as persons, we acknowledge that they have something to give, we provide them with an opening, or a channel, for their gifts, and we trust them enough to receive their gifts to us. We find our joy in letting *them* have the greater blessing of being the giver.

Building Bridges with Words

What does it mean, then, to *provide others with opportunities to give?* On the surface the principle seems simple: "Will you give me..." However, a deep plunge into this principle reveals that it is perhaps the most profound, if the most subtle, of the six.

This principle requires an activation of the throat center, of the power to put into words and give expression to *the reality we are creating* for ourselves in order that others might come to know it and interact with it, bringing to it their complementing gifts.

Each of us has the power to "name" our experiences. This is one very fundamental way in which we were created "in the image" of the Creator. At the heart of all great religions and teachings there is the knowing that the original act of creation was the sounding of a 'word.' "In the beginning was the Word." In the Eastern traditions it is taught that when the

101

"AUM" was spoken, all that is came into being. Human beings possess this power of the spoken word, the power to express our consciousness when 'subject' appears to be separate from 'object.' When we "name" our experiences, we assume our creative authority over them and take responsibility for them. (cf. Genesis 1:26-28, 2:19.)

Giving voice to our experiences not only brings them fully into our own consciousness on this 'objective' level, it also gives other persons access to them. No one can respond to our inner reality as we know it and experience it unless we give verbal expression to that reality. Our words are the bridge between our private worlds and those of others.

If we want to be totally loving, then, we will take responsibility for letting others know that what our experiences are in order that they might respond to us. Whenever we share of our private worlds, we *provide others with the opportunity to give to us.* We build a conscious bridge from ourselves to them in order that they might come into our life space if they choose to.

Let us say, for example, that you are newly married. As you experience her, your wife gets along better with people than you do. She has a lot of friends and is lovingly supported and enriched by her relationships. You, on the other hand, are withdrawn and unsure of yourself, finding it difficult to engage with other persons. Your wife is your only friend and companion. You are dependent on her for all your love, support and encouragement. You find yourself feeling hurt and threatened by her other friendships and fearful that you will lose her. The more hurt you feel, the more you withdraw and the less you are able to form other nurturing relationships.

First, it is important to acknowledge that there is no way your wife can know exactly what you are experiencing unless you tell her. She might guess, intuit, or sense what is going on, but she can't know how *you* are experiencing it nor to what degree you are conscious of it without the confirmation of your words. If you *create the reality* that "If she really loves me, she will be sensitive to how I feel" or, "If she were considerate and thoughtful, she wouldn't have other friends because of how much it hurts me," you will set yourself up to have *expectations* of your wife which can only lead to your disappointment and hurt.

An alternative is to take responsibility for **your own reality creation** by simply expressing it to her. You might tell her, "I'm really having difficulty with the fact that you have lots of friends and I only have you. I feel threatened and hurt when you spend time with and care for others. I feel I don't do well in making friends. I feel totally dependent on you for my love and support."

If you share in this way what you are experiencing, you will **provide her with the opportunity to give to you**, for now she knows what your reality is and she can respond to it.

When you give verbal expression to *your* experience, it is important to start your statement with "I" in order to stay in touch with your own creative center. If you say, "You hurt me" or, "You make me feel..." you give your creative power to your wife. You imply that *she* creates your reality. That leaves you helpless and at her mercy. By simply stating, "I feel hurt," you affirm in consciousness that you are in control of your own life energies and that you can choose to change your reality if you want.

By taking creative credit for your own reality, you also affirm your wife and leave her totally free to respond as she chooses. Implicit in your statements will be that (1) she is very important in your life and what she does matters a great deal to you, and (2) she is in charge of *her* life, but not yours. This makes you peers, rather then dependents or contenders.

Or, supposing you have a new job. Your boss is, as you experience him, a tyrant. He gives you orders as though you were his servant or slave; he shows no consideration for your feelings; he never bothers to explain anything to you, but rather simply gives you commands; he expects you to wait on him hand and foot.

First, it is important to recognize that your perception of your boss is entirely **your reality creation** and not a statement of "who he is" or even "what he is like." Reflected in your observations are your values, your preferences, your self-image, etc. To **provide your boss with opportunities to give to you**, therefore, you will need to sort out your judgments on him from your feelings about him and the needs you have of him. If he shows no consideration for your feelings, perhaps it is at least in part because you have never told him what you are feeling. If he never explains things to you, perhaps it is because you have never indicated that you want to know. Your willingness to let him in on your reality will determine the degree to which he has an opportunity to respond to you.

You might, for example, want to say to him: "I feel I would do a better job if I understood more fully why I am doing what you ask me to do. I would feel more a part of the whole, instead of feeling that what I am doing is meaningless." Or, "It would be helpful to me if I knew more explicitly what the responsibilities of my job are, instead of finding out piece-meal that you want me not only to take letters, handle orders and respond to customers, but also to make coffee, run errands and clean your office."

By telling him what would be helpful to you, you *provide him with the opportunity to give to you* should he choose to do so. Instead of passing judgment on him, and resenting him for *not* relating to you as you would like, you give expression to *your reality creation* to actively provide him with that opportunity.

Giving Expression to Your Private Reality

Simply stating what your reality is, then, is the first level of bridge building between you and another. You assume responsibility for making known what you are feeling, thinking, needing and wanting, and you do not assume that any other person will automatically *know* what your reality is.

This first step is especially important in close relationships. We are less likely to expect a near-stranger to know what we are feeling, thinking, needing and wanting than to expect a parent, child or spouse to know. Just because persons live with us, share common experiences, and love us does not mean that they share our reality creations. To the contrary, we remain unique and individualizing beings and share the intimacy of our private worlds only to the extent we are willing to reveal them to each other. If we want loved ones to respond to our deepest needs and wants, therefore, we will assume responsibility for verbalizing them, thus *providing the loved ones with opportunities to give.*

If you are married to a man you love very much, for example, and your life together is, on the whole, ideal, you may find yourself resenting the fact that he does not meet your needs sexually. "He should know me well enough to recognize that I need more holding, more tenderness, more time," you might be thinking. Meanwhile, because you have never told him what you are feeling and thinking, your husband may assume you *are* satisfied and never think to ask himself what more he can do for you. Or, he may sense that something is lacking in your lovemaking but not know what to do about it. Only if you tell him what you are feeling and thinking—give verbal expression to your reality—do you open the door to the new for *both* of you. Because he loves you, giving more to you will bring him deep joy. If you love him, you will *provide him with that opportunity.*

If you are an only son who has chosen *not* to take over the family business as your father had always hoped, but rather to pursue your own, quite different, career, you may feel that your father is disappointed in you, disapproves of the life you lead, and still tries to "run your life," or manipulate you, with allusions to how much he needs your help with the business.

You are perhaps more aware than your father is of the rather basic differences between the two of you, for *you* are the one who saw that business was not your niche in life. You, therefore, are more capable than he of putting those differences into words by sharing with your father what your reality is. You might say, for instance: "I find no challenge in business, as you do. It does not stimulate my creative energies as it does yours. I enjoy philosophical and religious inquiries far more— matters of the heart and mind. I feel like a fish out of water in business. I love you, Dad, but I am not *like* you in this regard and thus cannot with any freedom or joy follow in your business footsteps."

A simple statement may not be enough, but it will provide your father with an opportunity to engage directly with your reality and to share of his in response. From there, you can continue to strengthen the bridge between you as you give expression to more and more of your own experience of yourself, of him, of life.

Or, if your children are grown and have families of their own and you are now retired and alone, your spouse having died, you may feel lonely, useless, shunted aside. You may feel your children are ungrateful, because after all you did for them and gave to them over the years, they should be more considerate of you.

Instead of making assumptions about your children's motivations, or passing judgment on them, or feeling sorry for yourself, you could simply go to them and share your experience. "I'm feeling lonely, useless, shunted aside, like a used piece of clothing that is out of style. I don't feel a part of your life any more, and I don't have another life of my own. I am very unhappy."

Just by sharing your reality, you give of yourself to your children and you open the door to them to have a new relationship with you. You are not so much the parent now as a peer, inviting your adult "friends" to step into your inner world and bring their unique gifts to enrich you.

In all such exchanges, it is vitally important to *have no expectations but rather abundant expectancy*. If you try to determine in advance what response your sharing "should evoke," you are not building a bridge on which people can come and go freely in your life, but rather you are opening a trap-door which will lead to the ensnarement of an unsuspecting victim. If you "catch" your prey and your expectations are fulfilled, you may feel something still lacking—namely, the *willingness* of the other to give to you and perhaps even his or her good will. If the other does *not* fall for your 'bait,' you will not only feel disappointed, but you may find that you have put *yourself* in the trap and have a hard time getting out again.

If you give expression to your reality with *no expectations but rather abundant expectancy,* you will open a wide door to your inner being. You will build a verbal bridge across the chasm of your loneliness and sense of isolation, and stand on the threshold to see who is coming and what gift they bear. In your eagerness to share, you may even rush out to meet the other with open arms, embracing your invited guest, welcoming him or her and *receiving him/her as beautiful exactly where he/she is.*

Speaking the Whole Truth

Sometimes as we begin to give verbal form and shape to our inner realities, our private worlds, we have difficulty finding the right words. This is a clear indication of our sensitivity to the power that words have to express, and to bring into manifestation, that inner reality. It *matters* what words we use, because only the 'right' words will do. To search for the right words is to be a conscious creator, for once we give our inner reality the name that fits it, or fully expresses it, we are truly in command of it at a conscious level. For that reason it is important to keep searching until you feel the deep satisfaction of "Yes, that's it," when you say it.

This brings us to another facet of this verbal bridgemaking process which might be labeled "truth speaking." Because most of us live, to a large degree, in the private worlds of our feelings, thoughts, values and past experiences, there is little that can establish lifelines of communication between us and others except words. Words, which are merely labels we use to identify our experiences, become a medium of exchange in the area of communication just as money is a medium of exchange in commerce. By the use of words, we span 'time,' bringing our past into the present and projecting ourselves into the future. And we span 'space,' linking our private worlds with the *reality creations* of others.

Nevertheless, words are *not* the experiences themselves, but are only symbols of the experiences. To say, "My parents died when I was five" may be descriptive of the event, but it does not fully express your experience of it. Your reality includes not only the event, but what you felt and thought, and how much importance you gave to it. Therefore, you need to seek out word-symbols adequate to represent all facets of your experience.

In order to communicate the 'truth' of your experience to another, you would want to say something like: "My parents died when I was five. I felt abandoned by them. I thought they had died because they did not love me. That single event affected me so deeply that I have felt unloveable ever since and have been reluctant to trust anyone who says they love me." Or, "My parents died when I was five, but because I was surrounded by two very loving grandparents, two older sisters and an older brother, I never felt lonely. I was perhaps too young to miss them in the true sense of that word. I transferred my affection to other members of my family and felt no less secure, and if anything *more* loved, than before their death. My parents' death seems to have had no adverse effects on my life, and perhaps made me more aware than I might have been of the broad base of family love on which I stand."

To share your reality with another, to truly "put into words" what your experience is, you need to speak not only of events, but of your feelings and thoughts about them and of the importance you give to them. Only when you do, do you truly invite others to give to you, for only then can they know in truth what your reality is.

'Truth,' in this regard, has to do with matching your words precisely with the energy of what you are experiencing. Only you can know whether the words fit, and only you can experience the full flow of your life energy that results when you use the magic key of speaking truth to set yourself free from the prison of your own reality. It is perhaps for that reason that acts of 'confession' have been central to many religious rites and to the redeeming of ruptured relationships, for there is great life-giving power in speaking truth. Congruence between our inner reality and the words we use to express it, opens the channels of our being and enables us to give and receive freely. When we give expression to all that is going on in our private worlds, we release the life-giving force of our inner being which has been held captive in the unexamined, the unlabeled, the censored and/or the unshared.

This kind of truth speaking requires consciousness and self-knowledge, for in order to articulate what we feel and think, we must first *know*. Often it is as we seek to tell another that we discover just what an experience was for us.

For example, you share a confidence with a friend you feel you can trust. Later you find she has told a third party what you asked her to keep to herself. You feel angry, and call your friend to tell her off. As you begin to vent your anger, tears come to your eyes and you realize that what you feel is not anger so much as hurt. Tentatively, you say, "I think what I'm really feeling is very hurt, and perhaps betrayed." As your conversation goes on, and your friend responds to you, you realize that you set yourself up to get hurt by having *expectations* of your friend instead of simply *providing her with the opportunity to give* freely to you by asking, "If I tell you this, would you be willing to keep it to yourself?" What you in fact said was, "This is confidential, so don't tell anyone," not waiting to see if she agreed to your terms or not.

Your process of discovery in relation to your own *reality creation* has unfolded for you as you sought to put it into words by talking to her about it. You have come to see that it is not that you need to change your friend. Rather it is that you need to *be the change you want to see happen* by not sharing in the first place what you do not want to be passed on in the second place.

Learning to Set Yourself Free

On other occasions you know perfectly well what you feel and think, and what value you give to an event or a person, but because you pass judgment on your reality—deem it 'bad,' 'wrong,' 'unworthy,' 'sick,' 'strange,' or whatever—you never share it with others. You have 'labeled' the experience, but you are afraid to voice it for fear that verbalization will give it a power or reality that will somehow bring it into being—or, on the other hand, that will somehow ruin or destroy it all.

What you do not realize is that the reverse is actually true. By *not* giving voice to it, you give *your own reality creation* power over you: power to come and go as it pleases, power to separate you from other persons and thus to imprison you. You fail to take command of it by calling it by name and making it stand before you in the light of your full consciousness and the consciousness of another. Instead, you let it build up pressure within you until it "explodes" in some act of violence or destruction, or in some expression of such intensity that others cannot understand or relate to it. "Labeling" your experiences is not meant to create a prison for you to live in, but rather to build bridges between yourself and others.

For example, as a child you are beaten by your mother and sexually molested by your father. You grow to hate them both and begin to plot in your mind how you will one day kill them. At the same time, you tell yourself you are 'bad' to hate your parents and that God will punish you for having such terrible thoughts about them. You begin to think there must be something very wrong with *you*, since most people's parents seem to love them and relate to them kindly, whereas yours treat you like some kind of animal. You wonder if you deserve any better. This heightens your urge to kill. You are afraid to

109

tell anyone of your thoughts and feelings because if you do, you may discover that indeed you *are* less worthy than others, and perhaps even that you are going crazy.

Or, as a teenager you develop an intense crush on your English teacher. She becomes the focus of all your sexual fantasies and you daydream about secret encounters with her in which you both declare your love for each other. As the years go by, you cannot seem to get her out of your mind. It is as if you are obsessed by her. At first you do not tell anyone because you feel it is 'silly' that a high school crush should go on so long. Then you begin to worry about your mental health, for she is in your dreams frequently and she comes to mind almost any time you are with a woman. She has become a constant figure in your inner world—almost a symbol of sexuality. You would not dare tell *her* of your feelings, for surely she would laugh at you or ridicule you. Or, she might respond to you, and you wouldn't know how to handle that either.

Only as you put your inner reality into words that fully express the whole truth of it will you be able to take conscious control of it and make choices about how to release the energy that those feelings and thoughts represent. To build an energy bridge between yourself and another person is not only to provide you with a way *out* of your private-reality prison, but also to let others *in* that they might provide you with new perspectives and new experiences. Until you speak of your inner reality, you will live in fear of it.

Speaking the truth, then, is one of the most important keys to setting yourself free. The truth you speak is the truth of your own inner reality, your private world. You speak of what you know through your own experience. No truth spoken out of personal experience is absolute in the sense of being true for *all* people or for all time, but it is nevertheless your truth for this moment in time. If you give voice to it, you are free to move on from it and through it to new experiences, new discoveries, new truths. If you hold it within you, you lock yourself into the past, for you are continually focused on what was rather than what will next come into being.

Speaking the truth of your own experience, then, is a way of knowing yourself better and of taking conscious responsibility for your own *reality creation*. When you keep facets of your experiences hidden within, telling no one of them, you are the one who suffers from the imprisonment. You try to hide from yourself, but find that you alone have to live with the *reality creation* you find so horrible that you refuse to share it with others. Not only are you unable to love yourself completely under those circumstances, to *receive yourself as beautiful exactly where you are,* but you are unable to respond to your own needs, to your life circumstances or to other persons because of the restrictions and constrictions you have placed on yourself from within. And you are unable to receive the love gifts that others might be offering you.

You alone hold the key to your inner reality. You alone can determine whether you will make of your private world a castle of your own imprisonment, separated from others by a great dry moat of noncommunication, or if you will make of it a lovely garden of lush experience, open to the public for their own refreshment and discovery and enjoyment, with easy access provided by numerous bridges built from the garden out to the larger world.

To learn to speak the truth, the whole truth and nothing but the truth is to ensure your own freedom from the imprisonment of isolation and your access to the ongoing experience of your oneness with all others and the great nurturing and communion which that can provide you.

A Two-Way Bridge

A second level of bridge building between you and another might be called an invitation to exchange realities. Having shared what your experience is, you may want to *provide the other with opportunities to give to you* by sharing his or hers in return. As the newly-married man, for example, you might want to say to your wife, "How do you feel about friends? Are you as secure as you seem to me? Do you make friends as easily as you seem to? Am I central to your life? Do you feel as dependent on me as I do on you?" Or, as the new employee, you might want to say, "Have you felt satisfied with the work I've been doing, with the way we've been working together? Are there ways I could be more helpful to you?"

Once you acknowledge that no one can know what your experience is until you tell them, it is easy to see that the converse is true as well. You cannot know what others' experiences are unless they are willing to tell you. Therefore, to *ask* what they are experiencing is to indicate that you have built a two-way bridge. Not only are you willing to share what's going on with you, but you want to know their side of it, too.

As the wife who feels unsatisfied in your sexual relating, you might say to your husband, after sharing your reality with him: "And how is our lovemaking for you? Is there more I could do to bring you joy and satisfaction? Do you find our sexual engaging as fulfilling as you would like?" In this way you are not implying that there is something 'wrong' with him as a lover, but are instead exploring how you might find more joy together, through a joint effort.

As the son who does not choose to inherit his father's business you may want not only to express how your reality differs from your father's as you see it, but also to ask him to express his point of view. "Do you feel hurt because I've chosen a different profession, Dad? Are you worried about the future of your investment of time and energy and money? Do you feel left alone at this time of your life because you have no one to turn the business over to?"

Or, if you're a parent getting on in years, and feeling left out by your grown children, you might ask them, "What part do you feel I have in your life now? Are there ways I could be helpful to you and your family? Do you enjoy having me around?" The more direct and specific your questions are, the more you will find out that will be helpful to you as you seek to give your love more fully and freely to your loved ones and to yourself.

Your only son has just brought you home from the hospital to stay with him and his wife. You have had the latest in a long series of operations on your legs, severely damaged in your bout with polio when you were a young mother. You feel, once again, a burden—and a helpless cripple. Your son has never known you except in your handicapped state. All his life he has had to help care for you, since your husband left you alone with him when he was still small. Now you are bedridden. You worry that this added burden will be too much for John.

As he carries you through the door and into the improvised "guest room," you break down. "I feel so helpless," you tell him. "I don't want to be a burden to you, but I feel I am. I am afraid this will be too much for you to bear. I'm so sorry to be in the condition I am in," you sob.

You have built the bridge. Now, having given vent to some of your feelings, you indicate that the bridge is two-way. "Do you feel I am a burden, John? Is this too much for you?"

All your fears, worries and concerns can now dissolve in the rush of life-giving energy that flows from him to you. Now you begin to know what *is*. You can respond to that. As long as you were only *afraid* of what was, there was no way for you to engage at all.

"I'm afraid, too, Mother," John responds. His tears begin to flow, too. "At times I feel I *can't* bear the burden. I love you so much and I want to help you, but I hate to see you like this. It makes me angry. I feel you're wasting your life away. I wish I could make you well."

Now that you have both crossed the bridge, you can love each other more fully by exploring openly what each of you *can do*. Energies will flow more freely now that the feelings are unblocked.

Again, we would stress the importance of expressing only your own reality—starting your sentences with "I." If you want to know how the other feels, ask, rather than starting sentences with "you." Instead of, "You do too much for me," say, "I feel unworthy of all you do for me," or, "I don't know how to express my gratitude for (or how to return to you) all you do for me," or, "Do you feel you have to do more for me than you would like to, or have time or energy or money for?" Remember that you stand on only one side of the bridge and can only see things from *your* point of view. Don't try to speak for others. They have their own creative power of speech and can articulate their own realities far better than you could ever do for them.

We build conscious bridges to other persons, then, by taking responsibility for expressing in words the nature of our own experience, truthfully communicating our reality creations, and by extending the invitation to the other to exchange realities with us by sharing their experiences, by articulating their points of view. This is the most basic level of conscious bridge building.

Holding the Gateway Wide Open

Essential to the process of *providing others with opportunities to give* is determining how you will receive the gift that is given. Will you construct a tollgate at the access to your bridge, requiring some guarantee (some pay-off) before you let the other cross? This would certainly be to set up *expectations* which cannot help but limit the number of persons who will cross into your private world.

Will you make the bridge a drawbridge so that you can change your mind midpoint and deny persons access even after they have started to enter your private world? Or, will you stand guard at the other end of the bridge to take pot shots at the one who comes bearing a gift of self, to pass judgment and pronounce sentences? To do so would certainly not be to *receive all persons as beautiful exactly where they are.*

To fully practice this principle requires leaving yourself open to any gift that comes. If you hold a specific image of the gift you want to receive or the way you want it to be given, you are not really *providing others with opportunities to give,* you are making demands of them, or, at the least, laying your *expectations* on them. A *gift* is something freely offered. If you do not leave others free to give *their* gifts, then you are really asking for someone else to offer the gift that only you can give, to *be the change you want to see happen.*

To in truth *provide others with opportunities to give,* you must be ready, even eager, to receive what *they* will offer, not what you imagine or hope they will give. You must leave room in your reality for their free and creative expression, acknowledging and affirming their uniqueness, rather than asking them to conform to the limitation of your own. To do this principle is truly to open yourself to the depth and breadth that others can bring to your life.

For example, you are a member of your local school board, assigned as chairperson of a committee on interracial understanding in your community. Some of your committee members are opposed to what they call "racial mixing." Your initial response is to wonder why the president of the school board would appoint such persons to your committee, when it would seem their attitudes are contrary to the very purpose of the committee. Then, having taken several deep breaths, you realize that these persons are *not a problem but an opportu-*

114

nity, for you will have on your committee a full spectrum of viewpoints as you plan strategy for bringing about interracial understanding in your community.

At your first committee meeting, you *provide each member with the opportuniy to speak* at some length on his or her own feelings and thoughts about the need for and desirability of getting to know and appreciate persons who are of different racial and ethnic backgrounds from his/her own. As each talks, you listen carefully, wanting to understand as fully as possible the diverse viewpoints represented on your committee as a first step to understanding persons in the larger community. You probe with questions designed to elicit each person's *reality creation* as fully as possible. You do not invite discussion between members, but only urge each to make a full presentation of his/her own point of view and encourage others simply to listen and to receive those points of view. You practice *receiving all of the members as beautiful right where they are.*

At the end of two and a half hours, you have all heard a fairly comprehensive presentation of the attitudes and values, fears and hopes, stereotypes and images you will confront as you set out to expand racial understanding in the larger community. You feel blessed to have had such a wide exposure as preparation for the task you and the committee have before you. By *providing each member with the opportuniy to give to you,* you expanded your own understanding enormously and became better prepared to chair the committee.

Receiving Differences as Gifts

This principle springs out of the inner knowing that all persons are part of one large energy network called Life. No one person is more or less important than the other. Each is a connecting point in the entire network, at once no more important than any other and equally as important as all others. Each is essential to the harmonious working of the whole, and each represents a different time/space pinpoint of consciousness in the whole. None of us is complete without all others, and none of us can know other than our own point of view unless we open ourselves to other persons and the completion of the whole that they represent to us.

115

When you *provide others with opportunities* to come into your life, you are seeking to extend the boundaries of your private world to include the perspectives and experiences and talents of others. It is really their *differences*, then, that you welcome, rather than their sameness. If you approach them with *expectations*, you have only your past experiences to draw on and you fail to open yourself to anything beyond what you have already known. To open yourself with *abundant expectancy* is to welcome *whatever* comes, even—perhaps especially—the never-before-experienced, the heretofore unknown. It is in your experiences of the new and different that your own consciousness expands.

When others cross the bridge you have extended to them by your invitation to share, you have an opportunity to welcome them with open arms, *receiving them as beautiful exactly where they are.* Instead of viewing whatever differences they represent as *problems* to you, you perceive that they *are opportunities* to expand your own understanding of the life process.

It is important to receive fully the gift being offered before making a response to it, lest you react out of old habit patterns quite unrelated to the present engaging. To fully receive a gift, it is important to listen with full attention to what the other is saying *all the way through to the end,* breathing deeply all the while. Often, persons get ahead of the interaction by listening only to the first half of what someone is saying and then beginning to prepare a response. Thoughts about what you will say next cause static in your receiving set and you may not hear the rest of what the other is expressing. To fully receive is to let the entire gift in, to hold it, savor it, get to know it, *before* making any response. Focusing on deep breathing while listening will keep your mental and emotional energies moving, leaving you open and clear to continue to receive.

When you begin to receive in this full way, you may find you want to ask clarifying questions about what the other has said in order to be sure you received the gift he or she was offering. Only after becoming fully acquainted with the gift can you offer an appropriate response.

For example, you are a veteran of World War II. You fought in Europe against German troops and were among those to liberate Nazi extermination camps at the close of the War. You have always felt the United States was right to enter that war, that we helped stamp out an evil too despicable and horrible to imagine unless you smelled the burning flesh in those camps and saw the starving, brutalized human beings who somehow survived the Holocaust.

You have found it very hard to understand, let alone receive as beautiful, the young men of the '60's and '70's who speak of war as though it were piracy and of our armed services as though they were lawless brigands determined to loot the world no matter what the cost in human lives. One evening you find yourself at dinner with friends, and a young man in his mid-twenties begins talking of his work in what he calls the cause of "nonviolent social change." You recognize your opportunity to get on the inside of another *reality creation*, and so you *provide him with the opportunity to tell you* about his work.

He mentions the urgent need to change "the system." "Just what do you mean by 'the system'?" you probe. In elaboration he uses terms such as "military industrial establishment," "corporate power," "economic exploitation," and "the third (and fourth) worlds." Each time he uses such a label, you ask him to explain what he means by the terminology in order to let as much of his *reality creation* penetrate your consciousness as possible. You keep breathing deeply throughout, recognizing his experiences have been entirely different from your own.

At one point you ask, "What do you consider to be the formative events in your life as far as your political philosophy is concerned?" He points to the assassinations in the '60's of President Kennedy, Malcolm X, Robert Kennedy and Martin Luther King, to the Viet Nam War and the use of napalm on civilians, to Watergate and to the corruption of the FBI and the CIA. You begin to see that his experiences are not really comparable to your own, and you begin to understand that he could not possibly know, as you do, that wars *can* serve a positive purpose. He has only seen the negative, seamy side of power politics and international warfare. Naturally he would feel and think differently than you do.

You find you do not feel a need to convince him of your point of view, because you can see that each of you represents the learnings of your age and experience. Each of you is 'right' and is making an important contribution to the evolution of our nation's policy, both internal and foreign. Moreover, you find yourself hoping that he and his generation will, indeed, find an alternative to warfare as an effective means of bringing about change in the world. For though in your experience you have seen that sometimes war is essential, nevertheless, it *is* horrible and destructive beyond words. Nonviolence would be preferable if it were also effective against the warring intentions of other nations.

Having really listened, fully explored his reality and truly received his offerings as a gift to you, you are ready to respond freely and lovingly out of your own reality.

The response may be a simple, "Thank you." It may be an expression of appreciation for his act of giving. It may be that you will want to share how that gift has enriched your life, broadened your understanding, given you a new perspective. You may want to indicate how you will put his gift to use in your life. Or, you may want to share how your own reality differs from his, offering him in return the gift of your own experience. Whatever response you make, what is most important is the *receiving* you do first, for the one who gives will sense whether or not the life-energy, the love, which filled the gift has indeed been absorbed into your life space. If it has not, he/she will feel it return to him/her and will know that your invitation was somehow conditional and his/her gift has been rejected.

One of the most effective ways to keep bridges clear once you have built them is to give active, verbal praise and thanksgiving for everything and everyone that comes into your life. With each, "Thank you, Father-Mother of the Universe," or "I praise you, Lord of Life," or "I am *so* grateful!" or whatever words are meaningful to you, the bridges of openness are reinforced and the access way to your inner being is broadened.

Dealing with Specifics

Sometimes we provide others with opportunities to give in very specific ways, such as: "Will you please take the garbage out for me?" or, "I need to borrow $1,000 for a down payment on a house. Could you loan it to me?" or, "Would you go see my friend in the hospital and share some of your understanding about self-healing with him?" or, "Will you take care of my children today?" or, "Will you go to the movies with me?" or, "Will you introduce me to the head of your company?"

When you reach out to someone with a specific request it is especially important **not to have any expectations** as to what response the person will make, for when your request is specific, *whatever* response the person makes *is* his/her gift to you. A "No" is as much of a gift of self as a "Yes" is. Even in the "No" the other is giving you the gift of the truth of his/her energy flow in that moment. If persons cannot give you willingly and freely that for which you have asked, then to comply with your request would not be a gift of their love, but only an empty shell, devoid of life-giving power. If, on the other hand, they are truthful with you in saying "No" when that represents their true energy-flow, then they love you more in the no-saying than they would in "Yes." They also leave the door open to giving you a free-flowing gift of a "Yes" on another occasion when it is in harmony for them.

To **provide someone with the opportunity to give** in some specific way, then, is—if you are truly asking for a *gift* in love—to leave the door open to a "Yes" or a "No" as an equally loving response. If you do not really intend to leave persons the alternative of saying "No," you are not really providing them with an opportunity to give, but rather giving them directions or an order. It is important to be clear about the difference so that you can make your message clear. If you are meaning to say, "It is your responsibility to cut the lawn and I expect it done this afternoon," you are less than truthful if you phrase it, "You could give me a gift by cutting the lawn." Or, if you are meaning, "Don't wear my sweater," you mislead the other person if you say, "Would you mind not wearing my sweater?" Gift-giving is quite different from complying with orders, directives and explicitly assumed responsibilities. Both have their place, and they are quite different.

On other occasions, you will provide other persons with opportunities to take part with you in group projects or undertakings. Again, it is important to be clear about the nature of the invitation you are extending. If the project is clearly defined and others are being asked to carry out the designs already outlined, it is important to be specific: "We need people to take phone calls, address envelopes, go door-to-door, bake cakes, serve tables," or whatever. In such a case it is not appropriate or truthful to say, "What would you like to do to help?" or, "What do you think we should do?" On the other hand, if the project is in the planning stages, or there are no limitations on its expression, then you may want to say, "We need people to help with our project and whatever you can do will be greatly appreciated." If a free invitation is issued, it is important to stay open to the wide diversity of contributions that will come and of persons who will offer to take part. If you are not prepared to *receive all people as beautiful* in their responses, then be certain to limit your invitation to reflect your true intentions.

Another way you can *provide others with opportunities to give* is by making them aware of opportunities to give to persons other then yourself. This is a way of letting people know of job opportunities or avenues of service that await the gifts and talents of just such a one as they are, and is an open door to the sharing of specific talents with the larger body of humankind.

For example, you may know of an elderly person who needs a companion, of an opening for an artist at a local print shop, of a healing center looking for new cooks or therapists, of someone who needs a house and plant-sitter during a year's sabbatical, of a training program for paramedics, of a community forming that will focus on nonviolent training for and involvement in social action. By telling others of these opportunities, you may just open important doors they would otherwise not have discovered.

Similarly, it is possible to make *your* needs known to the universe at large, leaving yourself open to receive from whatever source is in harmony with the larger whole. This is *providing others with the opportunity to give* without knowing who the giver will be. It is leaving the door open to all sources.

For example, you need a job. You make your need known to the universe, releasing it from your inner being and knowing that it will be received and registered by the Source of all Being. Then you proceed to look for a job, putting in applications, telling all your friends and strangers alike that you are looking for work, responding to ads in the newspaper. You approach each day, each contact, each person, with **abundant expectancy,** for you know that your need will be met by the Universal Source. You just do not know how, or by whom, or when. Your responsibility now is to be out there looking, but with **no specific expectations** so that you do not limit yourself and/or miss the gift-response when it comes. Whatever is in greatest harmony for you at this time in your life will open up to you, of that you can be sure, and with gratitude you wait, not passively but actively, not in helplessness, but in eager hopefulness and **abundant expectancy.**

One of the most important ways we **provide others with opportunities to give** to us is by receiving them as friends, lovers, mates, children and parents. To enter ongoing relationships is to invite persons into your life space to share a large part of their **reality creation** with you continually. Such relationships can be enormously productive and growth-producing if you remember that when two become one, to whatever degree they do, they are twice as much as either was before the merging. It is because the other brings his or her uniqueness to you that you are enriched by such unions. Rather than responding to differences as irritating problems, therefore, you can rejoice in being able to have two or more viewpoints of life rather than just your own.

If each day you breathe deeply and open yourself to others anew, welcoming them in and **providing them with opportunities to give to you** of their uniqueness, you will be challenged and stimulated and stretched to the far reaches of your potential for flexibility, adaptability, growth, comprehension, and love. Then you will never grow old and neither will your relationships. Every exchange, from the most direct and physical to the most abstract and theoretical, to the most mystical and intangible, will be life-enhancing, and love will flow to you and through you in the same abundance with which it is given to you by the Universal Source.

To **provide others with opportunities to give** is to open yourself to more than your own private world. It is to experience your oneness with all persons and the richness of the One we all are.

Chapter Seven
HAVE NO EXPECTATIONS

The wonder and delight of *having no expectations but rather abundant expectancy* is that, when applied, this principle forever eradicates disappointments from your life. If you *have no expectations* you can't possibly be disappointed.

An *expectation* is a fixed view based on the past and applied to the future. It's as if we carry in our heads a small TV set on which we conjure up well-focused pictures of how something will happen, of what someone will say, of when something will transpire, of how someone will react, of where some event will occur. The *expectation* plays itself out on our screen and if we hold onto our image, we go out into the world expecting it to happen exactly as we saw it. We play our part true to the scripts we wrote in our own heads and wait for the other elements (people, places, events) to play their parts as well, as rehearsed, as dreamed up during our private *reality creation.*

Most often, the 'show' does not come off the way we planned it! We are disappointed. *How* disappointed we are depends on how much energy we had invested in having it come out exactly as we designed it. The more we invested, the more disappointed we are and the less open are we to what *is* actually happening.

For example: You are applying for a job. On your inner TV screen you see how you are dressed. You look wonderful. You see yourself arriving. You are greeted warmly, welcomed into the office, offered a cup of coffee. The prospective boss is friendly, interested in you as a person as well as in your ideas and creativity. Your previous background is almost irrelevant compared with how impressed he is with you as you are in the here and now. He asks you what you'd like to earn if you were to work for him. You see yourself lowering your head, humbly trying to come up with a fair proposal. You see the boss reaching across his desk toward you saying, "Now, now. Don't underestimate yourself." You are given the job at a fine salary and you see yourself starting the very next week.

You bring yourself *slightly* back to reality. You tell yourself that you may not be given the exact salary you'd like but you'll definitely be treated well and be given the job.

The morning of the interview arrives. You dress exactly as you saw yourself in the 'vision' and you *do* look wonderful. Off you go. There's hardly any traffic and you take this as a definite sign that all will go perfectly. You have a great deal of energy invested in things going as you wish. You really need this job. You enter the office and disappointment sets in almost instantly. None of the plushness you envisioned is present. A young girl is sitting behind a counter, mostly obscured from your view. You begin wondering if you are in the right place.

She's polite and warm towards you but you never even notice. You find it hard to focus on what is actually happening because you are mourning what isn't! She gives you an application to fill out. You do it, but you are resentful. You deserve more than this. More to the point, you planned on more than this!

A young man, young enough to be your son, you think unhappily, comes to get you. He, as it turns out, is your interviewer. You don't notice that he is personable, open and very interested in you because you are not open to him. He simply isn't what you expected, and you are so down that you hardly care about the job any more.

Because your enthusiasm has waned, you present less than you are to the interviewer and your chances for landing the job drop considerably.

In situations like this, your discouragement comes less from what is transpiring than it does from the disappointment born of your own expectations. By having expectations, you do your self a disservice. By wanting so badly to have happen what *you* want to have happen, you lose out on life as it *is* happening. You are so busy looking for what you planned that you completely miss what is.

There's a sense in which, by leaving the present and projecting into future, you actually end up living in the past, since when the future becomes the present you have brought your old ideas to it in the form of expectations.

An illustration would be planning in the present moment what you are going to say to a loved one tomorrow when the two of you meet. What you plan to say tomorrow (in the future) sounds good to you today. The morrow comes and you say, in the future which has now become the present, what you planned to say in the past, yesterday. You hear the words coming out and they sound stale, flat. You're not feeling them today with the same intensity, the same excitment as when you conjured them up yesterday. Further, you are missing out on the *now* again. You are focused on what you planned to say rather than on what is being evoked in you in the now moment.

An *expectation* is a limitation. By having one, you are setting restrictions on what will happen in a given situation rather than opening yourself to endless possibilities. By projecting ahead and expecting the result to match your vision, you limit yourself to your *own* input and to the *moment* in which the vision comes into being. Yet, as just illustrated, what you want on Monday and hope will come into being on Tuesday, may be totally wrong for you on Tuesday even though it was perfect when you thought of it on Monday! And it may take your interaction with another person to make that come clear to you. If you are closed off, boxed into your own expectations, you may never even come to see what is really best for you. You may deny yourself what you really want by locking yourself into what you *think* you want (thought you wanted.) In this case, even if your expectation is fulfilled, you are still a loser because you settled for the lesser when you could have had the more.

Returning to the scene with the loved one: After you said what you had previously planned, your friend/lover might have responded to that exactly as you might have dreamed and wished. You might have delighted in that and pursued further along the same lines. The interaction might have been perfectly satisfactory. Yet, what you missed was what might have happened between the two of you had you simply opened yourself to the now moment and proceeded with spontaneity, or not initiated at all (and especially not from the past) and waited instead to receive from your loved one, and to respond to what was coming to you. Something new and different, and *unthought of* by you, might well have transpired—in other words, the *more* that exists beyond expectations.

"Well, then," you might be saying, "does this mean that I can't ever plan anything or have goals or look forward to the future?" To the contrary. This principle *encourages* your forward-looking investment of energy. It's *how* you invest it that is crucial. This is where **abundant expectancy** comes in.

Abundant Expectancy

Living in **abundant expectancy** means looking forward eagerly, excitedly, openly. It means you are dreaming about something, planning for it, hoping for it, *and* that you are open to whatever form your dream, your plan, your hope, will take. You know *something* is going to happen. You simply don't know *what*, or how, or when, or where, or with whom. Rather than determining these factors ahead of time and demanding that they unfold as *you* want them to, you send forth your vision with **abundant expectancy** and wait to see how and if all the pieces fall together. Then, when the event occurs, you are delighted as well as surprised, because you are privileged to watch it all unfold before your very eyes.

In the job interview scene described earlier, **abundant expectancy** might have been applied in the following ways. You loved your vision of being treated royally, so you prepared yourself as in your vision and started out hopeful, yet open to whatever might happen. When you arrived, instead of being "turned off" by the tall counter and the hidden receptionist, you might have chosen to see this as evidence that this firm is careful in its screening process and doesn't waste energy on frills.

The youthfulness of your interviewer could have been seen as a sign of a liberal and energetic company that is more interested in quality than in age. If you checked back to your 'vision' of how things were going to go, you had that same quality represented by an interviewer who was more concerned with you and your creativity than with your previous experience. You picked up on the quality, but not quite on how it might present itself. By proceeding with **abundant expectancy,** you could have opened yourself to what was and to the unique ways in which what you desired was actually being presented.

In the scene with your loved one, you might have practiced *abundant expectancy* by sharing with the person that you were focusing in on him/her yesterday, and then sharing what it was you would have said yesterday had you been together. This would have disposed of an *expectation* quickly and put it in its proper perspective. Then you would have been free to proceed in the here and now moment with *abundant expectancy,* seeing what you were moved to say, receiving the other's response or his/her own expression in the now moment. It would have been like having your own cake and eating it too!

The major distinction between *expectations* and *expectancy* is in attitude and approach. Remember the adage that no person is an island unto self? We live together interdependently. In approaching life with *expectations* this precept is violated. We cannot live another's life. We have enough to do to live our own consciously! Hence, if you, for example, plan in your own head a meeting with another person and imagine what you will say and then how the other will reply, you are living life as an island unto yourself. You are doing all the participating—not only for yourself but for the other as well. About the only way you can make the transaction go exactly as you have planned is if you never engage with the other person. If you *go* to the other person, you may be very disappointed indeed. Once you engage with another, you must, by definition, allow for alterations and changes simply because an element other than your own planning unit has been introduced.

Though the example just given may seem basic and elementary, it is amazing how many times people are tripped up by this approach. A classic, real-life example of this is a high school teacher in Ohio who asked her class what they most enjoyed doing when it snowed in winter when they were little. One boy raised his hand and said "sledding." The teacher replied "Nooo.....," fishing for another answer. She had in mind a very specific answer and though she appeared to be asking an open question, she was doing nothing of the sort. The boy's answer did not fit into her lesson plan. No doubt at her desk the night before, she envisioned a perfect lead into the Hans Christian Anderson tale she was going to present as an example of a particular literary style, and she thought, "Now if

I ask them this question, they'll say ice skating, and we'll be right into it!" But "they" had their own answers and her plan was foiled.

The differing attitude and approach in proceeding with *abundant expectancy* is that although you might play out the entire conversation in your head prior to engaging in it with the other person, you are willing to let go of it all in an instant to allow for the exchange that actually takes place. Surprise is the wonderful element that is added. That surprise grows out of input *added* to yours in the midst of a living exchange, and in relation to your own remarks which may be totally different now—not only because of what is sparked in you but because you are a different person now than you were when you did the planning inside your own head, even if that was only a few minutes ago!

In this way, you come to the meeting with the person with preferences, very specific and enthusiastically sought preferences, but rather than being bound to them, you are open to whatever will happen and alert to the nuances as they unfold. Usually, you end up with a blend of what you wanted augmented and enriched by the other party.

Learning the Flow of Interaction with Life

While having *expectations* involves an energy investment that often ends in futility or disappointment, investment of energy in *abundant expectancy* enlivens every aspect of living. To live in *abundant expectancy* is to sit on the very edge of life's chair, alert to whatever each moment brings and ready to act on whatever is made available.

In *expectancy* you come to a situation with your hopes, dreams and goals. You combine those with what life is offering you in the now moment. As the two sets of perspective merge, the new commences. Coming to the very same situation with *expectations,* you are disappointed if they are not met and need to muster up the desire and the energy to let go of what you

127

thought was going to happen, see what actually did happen and how you feel about it, and *then* finally go on from there.

For example, you make all the neccessary arrangements to play a round of golf the day after a week of hard work. You are truly looking forward to the relaxation and exercise. You wake up on your golf day to the sound of rain. You are very disappointed. The forecast was for sunshine; your calendar was cleared; you left no room for anything to alter your plans. They lie in a wet heap at your feet. You feel your day is ruined. In that you left no room for alteration of your willed plans, you were functioning out of *expectations*. If you are stuck in the disappointment the rain brought, you throw a wet blanket on the rest of the day because you left yourself open to only one possibility.

If you had proceeded with *expectancy,* you would have looked forward to the day of play and when you awoke to the sound of rain you would have shifted gears quickly to ask yourself,"What else would I like to do today that doesn't require my being outside?" You would have been free to examine how you were feeling in the now moment and what would feel good to you as a special replacement gift for yourself.

Even when an *expectation is* met, there is really no way of determining whether the greatest success has been arrived at. You surveyed the situation from your infinitesimal vantage point and decided, based on your private world of feeling, thoughts and intuitions, what would be best for you. You focused on that, and by doing so no doubt helped to bring it into being through your concentrated imagining. Yet, you have no way of knowing what *more* there might have been for you because you didn't approach the scene with openness but rather with a pre-set idea. Had you allowed for more, you might have received far more. In settling for the lesser, for limitation imposed by your *expectation*, you satisfied yourself, but you have no notion of how much more may indeed have awaited you in the moment which cannot now be replayed.

For example, you plan an excursion to an amusement park. You decide when to leave, what shows to attend, with whom to go, and when to return home. Everything goes like clockwork. You have a lovely day. You determined how it would turn out and it did. You missed out on nothing—or did you? Everything went so perfectly that you left no room for any unknowns. Had you gone alone there's no telling who you might have met. Had you taken the bus instead of your car, you might have seen things along the way that were obscured by the concentration you invested in driving. Had you played by ear what show you would catch, you might have seen a nuance not present in the version you did see. Had you simply decided on an excursion and not predetermined the park, you might have stumbled on an adventure totally new to you.

Your exact *expectation* was met, but it constituted an act of completion as differentiated from one of beginning. The completion was "with *you* with you." You had the *expectation* and *you* had it met. Your interaction was with yourself, even while engaging with another in an experience of an 'outer' reality, namely the amusement park. Having completed your transaction with yourself, you might be ready to engage with the other and open yourself to what might follow. That is, if indeed you do and if it's not too late. The trap of *expectations* is that once they are met, the interaction often goes no further.

In *expectations* you are doing a solo; in *expectancy,* you come to dance as a partner with life.

Living in Harmony with the Larger Whole

Having an expectation is placing a demand on the life process. *Having expectancy* is asking the life process to show you what is in harmony for you. You may be asking for something which you would be far better off not having: a larger new car whose upkeep you can't afford; a big house which will require your constant attention; a promotion which will drain you and affect your health. Asking, rather than demanding, invites the universal consciousness to participate with you each step along the way. When steps fall into place with ease, you know you are proceeding in harmony. When stumbling blocks arise, *problems that are clearly opportunities* for your learning, you will fight against them if you have *expectations.* If you are proceeding in *expectancy,* you will acknowledge them as gifts from a loving Universe and reorganize your plans accordingly.

Perhaps you are wondering about whether or not you are to do a project on your own or submit it elsewhere. You begin to set things in motion in *both* directions—with the *expectancy* that the direction will come clear in its right time and especially if you do not impose your will on it. You submit the project elsewhere and begin your own work on it simultaneously. Both processes are tedious. The former because it takes weeks to get replies; the latter because your equipment necessitates a dual process that takes a very long time. You acknowledge the hangup in each case and proceed to do what you can, while continuing to ask to be shown the most harmonious way to go.

As a result of a windfall, sufficient money is made available for you to proceed with the project on your own. You are delighted. Yet, because you have had *no expectations,* you do not receive this as a completion. Rather, you wonder what more might be in store for you. With your senses alert to all possibilities, you set in motion the necessary steps to complete the project. In the midst of your efforts, another large sum of money is made available to you. This opens the way for you to inquire about the purchase of a new electronic device which will cut your labor time in half. You never would have 'thought' of this if you had tried to plan each step along the way in advance, but because you were open to the more, the more became available to you. As things happen, in the harmony of the Universe, your old equipment is sold immediately and the excellent price you receive for it brings exactly what you need to complete the purchase of the new model *and* pay for the project itself! During this entire project, you proceeded in *abundant expectancy.*

Now let's look at a second instance, one which involves proceeding in *expectations.* You have the possibility of doing a project for someone else. You have yourself convinced that you are proceeding with *expectancy.* Yet, you are stymied at so many turns along the way, and you invest so much energy in justifications of those blockages and in attempting to explain them away so that you can get on with what *you* determined you would do, that even *you* have to see the error of your ways after awhile. Hardly anything goes right with the venture, no matter what you do to redo what wasn't working. Had you proceeded in pure *expectancy* in the beginning, you would never have gotten in as deep as you did.

Going Into the Fertile Void

Vital to being able to create a lifestyle of living in *abundant expectancy* is coming to know the Fertile Void. The Fertile Void is the empty space in our lives in which nothing exists of the past, or of the present and future, for that matter. The Void is like our own private wall-less room, boundless like the Cosmos itself, where life-substance flows unconfigurated in illumined darkness. It is the haven where you can bide your time, where nothing is asked of you, where—ironically—you are *encouraged* to do absolutely nothing. It's where you 'go' when you don't know what to do in a given situation and rather than revert to old tapes and wornout behavior, you choose to do nothing until something new becomes clear to you.

It is in the Fertile Void, in the privacy and intimacy of your own inner self, that you may strip down to the core of yourself, shedding the garments of previous *expectations* of yourself and exposing yourself to the new like a newborn child in a world of wonder.

The time in the Fertile Void is different for each person. It varies with what is under consideration. A person might spend *years* in the Fertile Void on one matter, only moments on another. The purpose for entering the Fertile Void is to allow a clear, intuitive direction to emerge rather than thinking up (based solely on prior experience) a way to go. Prior experience does not necessarily lead you to the new: often it merely is a rejuggling of the old.

The new is less a thoughtful rehashing or an idea-to-try and more an inspiration, a surprising way to perceive or respond. It often happens, for example, that persons arrive at a juncture in their lives when they no longer wish to continue to engage sexually. This can be very difficult to deal with if the individual is in a relationship in which the mate is still desirous of engaging sexually. If the person-ready-for-change (let's take a woman as an example) has *expectations* of herself, she may kill off her chances of allowing the new to emerge. In this case having *expectations* would manifest as 'buying into *realities created by others.*' They would run something like: 1) a woman my age is *supposed* to want to engage in sexually, 2) if you love someone you want to have sex with him, 3) there must be something wrong with me; maybe I'm becoming frigid, 4) maybe I'm becoming a homosexual, 5) I must cure myself of this right away.

To enter the Fertile Void is to let go of such *expectations* of self. It is to cease asking, "What's wrong with me?" and to open self to what is right, to what new may be coming into being. It is to give up thinking of ways to cope or of solutions. It is to cease condemning self for being different—not only from others, but from the way you used to be. It is to abandon the rush-to-resolution and to be willing to step out into the unknown instead.

To enter the Fertile Void is to give up trading an intolerable situation for equally intolerable solutions. Sometimes persons will go to a doctor for cure of an illness they have convinced themselves they have, when what they have is a good case of change knocking at the door. Sometimes persons will give up what's not working for them in one arena and try it on in another—such as rushing off to have an affair to get their sexuality working again and finding they have simply carried their problem with them to the new bed—or they arrive at the false conclusion that this handicap is their new lot in life—in effect giving up and not looking at all for what the new might be.

Entering the Fertile Void is to let go of all that, to arrive empty and remain that way until filled from within anew.

If the woman no longer wanting sex enters the Fertile void, she ceases engaging sexually and has the opportunity to lovingly share her process with her mate. She does not 'prostitute' herself by 'servicing' her husband. She gives him the gift of herself by being true to who she is. She waits *however long* for the new expression to emerge. When it comes there is no mistaking it. The pathway for bringing the new into being opens with ease and is scattered, as it were, with velvety and fragrant petals of the springtime of a budding beginning.

The new might manifest in a continuous high that replaces the stop and go nature of sexual orgasm. It might result in a whole new way to relate not only to her mate but to others as well—a way in which it becomes possible to love all persons equally, universally, without the stickiness of personal attachments. To allow new insights such as these to emerge it is imperative to give self a time of nothingness rather than a rush of judgment.

The key quality of the Fertile Void is its vastness, its nothingness. It is a corridor of question marks which dance haphazardly together to the refrain, "I don't know where I'm going." After a time, sometimes very long, their movement forges into a newly-choreographed expression and leaves the dark backstage wings of the Fertile Void to make a smashing debut in the spotlight of life.

The most necessary ingredient in the Void is *abundant expectancy.* One must be actively searching, alive and tingling with eagerness, ready to greet whatever comes into being with a rakish tilt of the head and a gleam in the eye.

The Fertile Void is the birth chamber where we are permitted to be a fetus all over again in relation to each new phase of our lives.

None of us knows what is going to happen in the next moment. Nor do we know if what we think we want to happen is what is best for us. About all we know is what *is* happening in the moment we are living it.

Living in *expectancy* enables us to live in the now, now.

Planning for the Future

Having no expectations and waiting in the Fertile Void does not mean that you cannot make plans or set goals. The plan or the goal is *not* the *expectation.* The *expectation* is your investment of energy in *how* the goal will come to fruition, in how the plan will unfold, in what the visible results will be. The plan or goal may indeed become a reality, but you may miss the sweet success because you were so fixed in your own view of the particulars that you never did see what actually transpired.

For example, you studied long and hard to be an engineer. You had a dream focused on a particular company, and visions of an excellent salary with good benefits and of admiration and appreciation danced in your head. You got your degree but no job. You are frustrated and angry, determined that you *will* find a way to get hired by the company of your choice.

In the meanwhile, you accept an invitation to join a newly-forming community in which your skills are very much in demand and you are highly respected. You go to live in the community. You do the work you are prepared to do and feel challenged by the tasks you undertake. All your financial needs are met, as well as your health care, and the community provides your housing. But you are not happy. You are biding your time. You are still seeking your ideal, your private world image of how it should be. What you are missing is that all you dreamed of, you have in a different form—respect, security, abundance. By longing for what *isn't*, you are missing what *is*, and stifling your own creative contribution for want of the more you expected.

Or, you are stricken with a heart attack and your *expectation* is that you will fully recover and return to your former state of health and capacity. You *do* heal, but not as you thought you would. You can no longer live at your former pace; your body requires you to slow down and temper your activities. You become despondent. Your healing has not met your *expectations*.

If you had been functioning in *expectancy*, you might have opened yourself to the blessing and meaning of the healing that *did* occur. You might have seen that rather than return to an old state of health, you moved to a new and more efficient one. Now, as differentiated from previously, you have a built-in checker or pacer of your energy expenditure. Your heart is going to serve you by telling you instantly what you can and can't do in a given moment, and hence keep you from pushing yourself into a danger zone. The healing did indeed take place, and with a bonus besides.

The trick to seeing the more as you proceed with your plans for the future, is functioning in *expectancy*—eagerly seeking the new, the deeper meaning, the unexpected.

Look for the New
Having no expectations can be practiced daily. Let go of the image you have of persons you think you know intimately and look to see who they are each time you engage with them. Awake in the morning and allow yourself to peruse all the plans you've made for the day, especially the "must do's." Then say about them all, "If they are in harmony!" Now you still have your plans but you have introduced the element of release. If something doesn't come off as planned, look to see what new *opportunity* awaits you, or what time was freed up and for what you might wish to use it, given this new moment to reflect on what's going on with you.

Go to routine places, like work or school, with the question alive in your head, "I wonder what new will happen today?" To look for it is to see it. 'It' is always happening whether you are oblivious or aware.

Awake with gratitude and excitement, as if you had a whole day to yourself—because indeed you do. Live in very *abundant expectancy.*

THE LOVE PROJECT PRINCIPLES
and
THE SEVEN ENERGY CENTERS

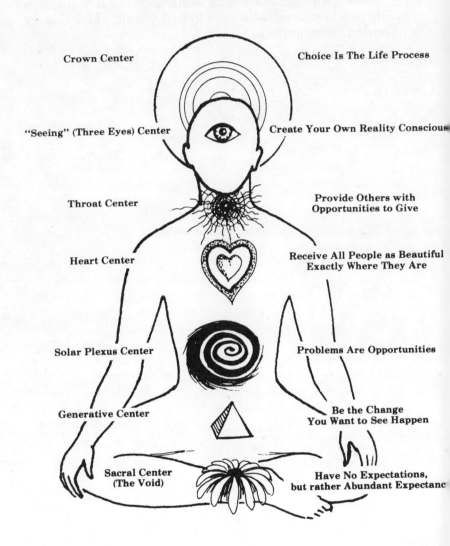

Crown Center

Choice Is The Life Process

"Seeing" (Three Eyes) Center

Create Your Own Reality Conscious

Throat Center

Provide Others with
Opportunities to Give

Heart Center

Receive All People as Beautiful
Exactly Where They Are

Solar Plexus Center

Problems Are Opportunities

Generative Center

Be the Change
You Want to See Happen

Sacral Center
(The Void)

Have No Expectations,
but rather Abundant Expectanc

Chapter Eight
THE SEVEN ENERGY CENTERS AND THE LOVE PROJECT PRINCIPLES

As human beings we have the distinction of being complex energy configurations rather than simple, one-dimensional and predictable 'objects.' When we identify ourselves with the cosmic coding "I AM," we mean far more than what would be communicated by the one-celled amoeba. Our "I AM" refers to an interconnecting web of shadings and modulations, of meanings and expressions. As human beings, we are many-facets-in-one. The more we know about each of our facets and shadings, the more we come to know the larger "I AM" of which those facets are an expression and the less we are identified with or locked into any *one* of them.

How many times have you said things like "I am a person who... is very stubborn, or cries at the drop of a hat." Each time you make a statement like that, you are identifying the whole of yourself with a single facet. The stubbornness may be related only to mind-sets you have developed; the easy tearflow to a solar plexus sensitivity. In both cases you are describing facets of yourself and not the whole.

To know when you are channeling energy through a particular facet of self is to create a climate of awareness in which you can easily and fluidly make *choices* about the quality and intensity of your particular expressions. We want to share with you here about the seven energy centers in your energy field in order that you might be able to identify the various facets and shadings of your interactions and *make choices* in greater awareness.

Human Energy Fields

Long ago Paul of Tarsus wrote: "Now we see only puzzling reflections in a mirror, but then we shall see face to face. My knowledge now is partial; then it will be whole, like God's knowledge of me. In a word, there are three things that last forever: faith, hope, and love; but the greatest of them all is love." (NEB I Cor. 13:12-13) Truly, in this phase of our enfoldment that we call 'objective' or 'self'-consciousness, most of us most of the time do not see the energy world directly, but rather we see through the 'mirror' of our mental images. Our consciousness is focused on abstractions from the energy we register with our neural system, light-rays reflected off the 'things' we see. (cf. Chapter Two, pages 8-10.)

So it is that in our interactions with other persons and with the events of our lives, we focus primarily on what we *think* is happening (the images we hold in our private worlds of what is happening) rather than on the actual *energy* that is moving, flowing, in us and through us, and between us and every 'other,' linking us together in one inseparable, dynamic reality. However, one day we will be able to perceive the energy-world itself, directly—not through the mirror-images held in our mental world. That will be the seeing "face to face" of which Paul wrote. With that clear seeing will come full knowlege of the world in which we live.

In order to point you beyond your private world to that real energy-world in which you actually live and move and have your being, we would like to offer you a 'road map' that has been very helpful to us: a description of our human energy fields and how they function. The description cannot, of course, give you an *experience* of your own energy and the energy of other persons or things, just as a road map cannot give you the journey it represents. But it can inform you of what awaits you and perhaps entice you out of the comfort and security of your private world into the thrilling and expansive direct experience and perception of yourself and others *as energy*.

The modern sciences of mathematical physics and quantum mechanics have been establishing through various scientific formulas, proofs and demonstrations what perceivers of Truth in all ages have seen directly: that there is no difference in basic makeup between what we used to call

'physical' and 'spiritual,' or 'matter' and 'energy.' *All* is
energy, and what appears to us as 'matter' or 'physical' is only
energy vibrating at very slow rates.

Scientists have gone far in their exploration of the energy
world of the 'unseen'—realms where molecules are moving at
such rapid speeds that we cannot see, hear, touch, smell or taste
them with our senses geared to the 'material' or 'physical'
plane. They have established that everything functions, in
fact, within an autonomous field of energy having its own
unique pattern formed by the lines of force which define it.

We would like, now, to direct your attention to your own
autonomous field of energy. The road map we offer you can be
found described in Eastern philosophies and other ancient
sciences of being. We have allowed this discription to unfold in
our own consciousness through direct experience of the
'territory' the map represents; therefore, what we present is our
own *reality creation* in relation to the seven chakras in each
human energy field.

Seven Energy Centers, or Chakras

Just as light refracts , upon passing through a prism, into
seven color rays, so the force or energy which gives you 'life' is
refracted by your consciousness into seven wave-bands of
energy waves and frequencies which are called *chakras* in the
Sanskrit, meaning a "center" or "wheel" of force. Those seven
energy centers are like frequency bands on a radio set. Impulses can be sent or received on them and transmissions can
be singled out from among the many being sent on the various
frequencies available by tuning in your set to a given wave-
band.

In each of our human energy fields, seven wave-bands can
be delineated, enabling us to sort out our experiences and more
clearly and consciously perceive what energies we are sending
and receiving. Each chakra is characterized by qualities
which differentiate it from the others. Thus, just as one can
learn to perceive the difference between the hues of color
characterizing red and orange or blue and indigo, so one can
learn to distinguish between the qualities which characterize
solar plexus energies as contrasted with heart center energies,
or those of the three eyes center* as contrasted with the crown
chakra.

---

*Often called the 'third eye' center.

As you practice discerning the differences between the various energies registering in your consciousness, you will better be able to live a balanced life of love in which your whole being is actively expressing and responding in an open flow and interchange with the energy world in which you are integrated.

The energy centers are not *in* the body, they are *of* the autonomous field of which your body is a representation on the 'physical' or 'material' level of frequency vibration. Your body is one facet of your autonomous field, and is itself a dynamic configuration of energy. Most of us relate to our *images* of our bodies rather than to the energy they actually are. Nevertheless, because most of us are more sensitive to our bodies than we are to other facets of our energy fields, it is often helpful to correlate the seven chakras with parts of the body identified with them, and we shall do that here.

No energy center has greater value than any other. Hence, you are not 'more evolved' if you are channeling more energy through one particular center and 'less evolved' if your focus is on another. Any distinction between 'higher' and 'lower' in reference to the chakras has to do with the vibrational qualities (greater or lesser number of waves per unit of time) rather than with any implication of moral judgment that one or another is 'better' or 'worse.'

Each center performs a specific and irreplaceable function as regards energy distribution and expression. Each is as important to the whole as is the other. Each works in conjunction with the others, and when we are whole and in balance, all seven are open and flowing with equal force.

We are known by our works, by what we manifest in the 'physical' world. *What* we manifest is a composite of how we align the energy as it flows through the seven chakras.

The Polarities

Every energy field is characterized by a positive and a negative pole which, in their contact with each other, their union, establish the lines of force of the field and hold the pattern which characterizes that field. At the heart of each atom, for example, an electron (negative) and a proton (positive) unite to form the single-unit, powerful field we call an

THE AUTONOMOUS FIELD:

**Lines of force created by
energy arcing between the
two poles.**

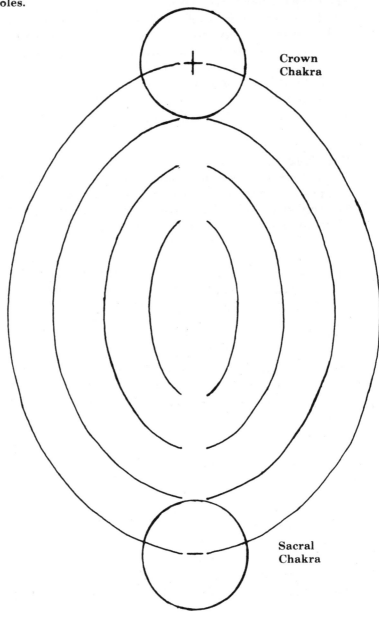

Crown
Chakra

Sacral
Chakra

atom. So in the human field there are two polarities, mirrored on the 'physical' plane in the ovum (negative) and sperm (positive), which are labeled the Sacral Chakra (negative) and the Crown Chakra (positive).

Each autonomous field, or 'human being,' is established by a flow of energy between those two polarities. In our objective state of consciousness we are relatively unaware of the functioning of this aspect of our being and of the qualities that characterize the force which defines our fields. Those who intuitively sense the energy flow between the two polarities often speak of it as a "higher power" or "God."

The Sacral Chakra

The negative pole of the autonomous field which gives you form as a human being corresponds to the base of the spine in your physical body. It is known as the sacral, or root, chakra. We shall also refer to it here as the "Fertile Void."

The sacral chakra represents the unknown in your life, that which will, in its own time, come into being, into form, into manifestation, and thus into your own consciousness. When first you begin to register the energy frequencies of this chakra in your consciousness, you may well talk about them with such words as trust, faith and/or hope—those great and lasting qualities Paul wrote of in the passage quoted above that are second only to love. You will develop an awareness that what is about to unfold in your life is already in process. That you are provided for. That you do not need to worry about tomorrow, for it will take care of itself. A fundamental trust in the life process of which you are a part, a sense of confidence that all will be well without your needing to do anything to 'make' it happen through your own efforts, emerges as you become more and more conscious of the sacral energies.

The sacral chakra represents your pure potential to be, to become, to manifest anything and everything. In the Fertile Void represented by this chakra, energy 'substance' waits to be brought into form and shape. You will discover, as you activate these energy frequencies consciously, that you are an individualizing expression of the abundant, infinite potential of the cosmos to become and to be. You will feel enveloped by a warm 'darkness' much like being in an energy womb, for Life

142

surrounds and fills you in this Fertile Void, providing nourishing substance for the hunger of the new, the More, which is waiting to be brought into being by you and through you.

The Void represents the experience of waiting, but not of inactivity. To activate the sacral energies is to experience a time of quiet restlessness. Like a mother carrying a child in her womb, you can actively nourish yourself with reading, companionship, exposure to new thoughts, activities, places and spaces, but there is no way to hurry the process of becoming, or to force the birth of the new before its time. Nor can you know exactly when it will come or what form it will take until it has come full term.

The **Love Project** principle *have no expectations but rather abundant expectancy* is an active way to bring the sacral energies into your consciousness. *Expectations* are based on the past, rather than on the new which is to emerge. By letting go of any specific images or ideas of what might emerge in the future, you clear your energy field for what is yet to come. The attitude of *abundant expectancy* is the turning of your awareness to the activity taking place in the Fertile Void. It is an affirmation of the life force that is moving there, and an opening of your consciousness to whatever will emerge.

All *expectations* are based on past data. In the Void there is no data. There is only energy in its pure, unconfigurated form igniting itself, alerting the other chakras to prepare for its arrival, enlightening the whole self by the rays of dawning it emits from its cosmic womb.

Having no expectations is a way of rendering the Void free of limitations, of allowing the new expression to develop as it will rather than ladening it with your past memories or with your future wishes (which also eminate from the past) as you seek to fulfill old, as yet unmet, desires.

The Fertile Void is virginal. Each time it is penetrated it is as if for the first time. In the Fertile Void there can be no predictability as to outcome. If under similar circumstances, once before, you experienced a sense of being on the brink of something and it manifested in a new relationship, you cannot have the *expectation* that the same is in store for you now. To have that *expectation* would be to dampen the flame of the sacral energies and to lengthen the process of germination.

Expectancy is *as* important as the having of *no expectations.* It is a saying "yes" to the process, an activating of awe and wonder in relation to the star in the east calling your attention to the new birth which is coming in you. To ignore the process is as hampering as attempting to squeeze the emergence into an outdated, illfitting form.

The energy of the sacral center can be activated in your consciousness in relation to your life in general by developing the openness and eagerness of a child, viewing each day as a vast playground to explore. To call up the life force beyond the surface of your skin is to activate it in your entire autonomous field. You will begin to feel that all things are possible for you, that no goal is too big to undertake, and no obstacle large enough to stifle your creativity.

To live your life within the security of the Fertile Void is to know that under all circumstances you are protected because you have available to you just the resources you need for the meeting of all eventualities. Therefore you can dare all, risk all, and rest assured that the new which awaits you will bring you the joy of experience, understanding and creative self-expression.

In specific life situations, you can activate the sacral energies by letting go of your limiting perceptions of what is going on and where it will lead you, and by opening yourself to new insights, understanding, feelings, courses of action and words to speak. Thus you will never lose touch with the element of surprise in your life—even when you are troubled. Trusting whatever process you are engaged in, you will be able to leave yourself open to grace—to gifts of the new in each new moment.

To live in *abundant expectancy* is to be a living meditation. Focusing your consciousness on the sacral energies, you lift your forces up and bring them to 'meet' the energies of the opposite polarity—the Crown Chakra. If you hold yourself in alertness, asking for the new gift that will be given and waiting with a hopeful heart, you will, in your not-knowing, remain confident that when you do come to know what will be, all will be well. Thus you will live in joy and gratitude even as you wait, and as you receive each new gift, you will know far More awaits you, for your potential, like the cosmos, is limitless.

144

**The Activated CROWN and
SACRAL CHAKRAS in the
Autonomous Field**

Crown
Chakra

Sacral
Chakra

The Crown Chakra

The positive pole of your autonomous field corresponds to the area just above the crown of your head. It is known as the crown chakra.

When you begin to register the energy frequencies symbolized by the crown chakra, you will more than likely experience them as the revealer of all things, for you will *know* what is. It is for that reason that you lift the sacral energies, symbolized by the darkness of unknowing, to the crown energies, symbolized by the light of knowledge. The light illumines the darkness and what was only potential takes form in your consciousness as that which has been revealed or made known.

As you practice bringing the crown chakra energies into consciousness, you will know more and more clearly what the perfect pattern of your life is, as defined by the lines of force of your autonomous field. You will know what decisions are in harmony for you, what course of action to follow, what relationships to pursue and which to let fall away. You will know all you need to know for the living of your life.

To activate the crown center energies is to stand in the light to have the now moment illumined. Whatever is unknown will be made known to you, whatever question you ask will be answered, whatever guidance you seek will be given.

The crown center energies generate activity. They end the time of waiting and bring the quickening of the new. When these energies enter your consciousness, the new direction, the new form to which you are to give birth, will be so clearly revealed that you will have only to do it. Your way of proceeding will be clear. The divisiveness of self-doubt will fall away.

It is for this reason that many refer to these energies as "a voice" which speaks, gives guidance and direction, tells them what to do—the "still, small voice" that is "God within." So clear will these energies make your knowing, it will be as if you have been spoken to by the God-Force Itself—and indeed you will have been, for your Higher Self, your autonomous field, is an individualizing expression of that universal power.

You will know all you need to know for the living of the moment in which you find yourself, and in the knowing, power will be released—enough strength for the task at hand, grace sufficient for the day.

The two polarities meet and merge in each here/now event of consciousness. Thus you never give yourself more than you need in the given moment. This is the truth symbolized by the manna God gave the Israelites in the desert. The light and truth which feed you, nourish you, strengthen you today, cannot be held in reserve for the morrow. What energy and insight you are given is yours to use, to spend, in the activity set in motion by the gift of crown center awakening. But just beyond the circle of knowing that lights your way, you are couched in the dark womb of unknowing that you might once again step out in total trust, in faith, for the potential awaits you ever fresh, ever abundant. The new *will* be given. The knowing will once again dawn at the coming of the new day or in a moment of need.

To practice the conscious registry of crown center energies, therefore, stay focused on the here/now of your everyday life. Do not ask what you will become; *be* who you are today. Do not ask for guidance to illumine the rest of your life; seek to know the step to take as you make your way through this hour, this day.

Hold in your consciousness always both the knowing *and* the unknowing, the sacral and the crown center energies. The choice you make today can be changed tomorrow in the light of new understanding born of the experience you are having today. Entrust the results of each act, each word, each thought, each feeling to the Fertile Void in **abundant expectancy** in order to learn from the decisions you make. Your learning, digested with **no expectations,** will be woven into the strong web of tomorrow's sure course of action.

For **choice is the life process,** and in each new moment of awareness—in each new registry of the light of crown chakra energy frequencies—you are free to make a new choice. You are free because you are not bound by the past, as you would be in **expectations,** but rather are embraced by the warm openness of the Fertile Void. Poised on the tiptoes of **abundant expectancy,** you are free to choose the next perfect step for you the moment it is shown.

Once you have brought the awareness of these two stabilizing polarities into your consciousness, you need never flounder in doubt again. When you do not yet know what to do or say, or how to proceed, affirm your experience of the Fertile

Void. Remember that *all* things are possible to you, but you can seize only one possibility, one opportunity, at a time. Wait in **abundant expectancy** to see which single one is in harmony for you in *this* here/now moment. When you do not yet know, give gratitude that you will, and wait.

When the knowing comes, act with confidence and self-assuredness, going quickly about the business the Father-force has given you to do. But acknowledge that you know *only* what you know and that what you know is *only* for you. And remember also that your time of not-knowing will return. Thus you can act in true humility—knowing that you know, rejoicing in your knowing, and knowing that far more vast is what is yet to be revealed to you.

To function in conscious awareness of the sacral and crown center energies is to know your Higher Self. Your Higher Self *is* the autonomous field described by the lines of force which course between the two polarities. Your autonomous field, or Higher Self, is a microcosmic expression of the cosmic pattern of unfoldment. Your Higher Self, to use familiar language, is God at work in you: the crown chakra is the Father-force active in your field, the sacral chakra is the Mother-force (what Christians have long called the Holy Spirit), and your personality self, defined by the remaining five chakras (which we will describe below) is the Son in the holy trinity—God incarnate, made flesh, and dwelling with us.* To be conscious of your autonomous field, your Higher Self, is to live in the constant presence of God, under 'His' guidance and protection, and to know that you are one with that life-giving cosmic force.

Your Personality Self

Your personality self is a particular time/space configuration brought into being and given expression by your autonomous field, or Higher Self. It is an individualized pattern of self-expression, integrated in a particular racial and cultural group at a specific time in history, and further

---

*On another level, your autonomous field is the "son" in relation to the larger, cosmic, Father-Mother Force.

THE PERSONALITY SELF and
THE FIVE CHAKRAS OF
MANIFESTATION

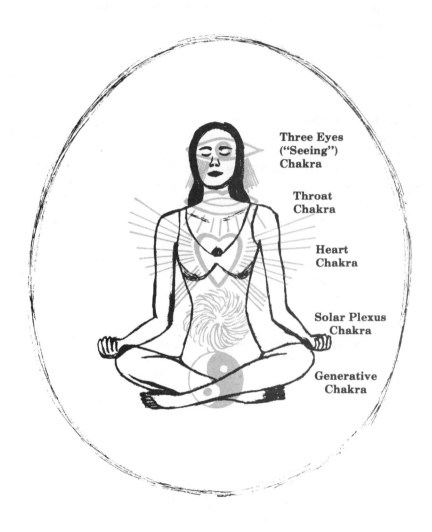

Three Eyes
("Seeing")
Chakra

Throat
Chakra

Heart
Chakra

Solar Plexus
Chakra

Generative
Chakra

identified with smaller groups and spaces called families, cities, states, nations, religious affiliations, and volunteer associations. Your personality self is that expression of your consciousness which is readily identifiable by other persons as your 'physical' appearance and the qualities which characterize the person you have been and are becoming. Your personality self has a given name.

There are five wave-bands of energy frequencies on which you 'broadcast' who you are as a personality. It is to those five energy centers that we now turn our attention.

The Generative Chakra

The lowest, or 'slowest,' energy frequency at which you give expression to your personality self and receive energy transmissions from others is symbolized by the generative chakra. It corresponds to the genitals in the 'physical' body and has to do with those energy frequencies we identify as 'physical,' or 'material.'

This wave band is no doubt the most familiar to you, for you sense it and respond to it with your five so-called 'physical' senses. The energies of the generative chakra are those on which you bring into being and respond to 'physical' forms, such as 'physical' bodies and/or objects of art, science and technology.

This is the center of creative action through which you are able to *be the change you want to see happen.* You can literally bring into being, into expression, into form, whatever you choose, for from the center of your own creativity you can generate whatever 'thing' or reality you wish. If, however, you spend your energies trying to get someone else to bring into being what you want to see take form in the world, you make yourself entirely dependent upon the other person's creativity, awareness, and choice-making. You, in that case, do not generate the new yourself, and do not bring it into being in your own energy field. Instead you abdicate your creative potential by letting your generative seeds of new life-expression spill on the ground of your being. To *be the change you want to see happen* is to fulfill your creative potential and to offer the unique and wondrous gifts of your own individualizing being to the world.

150

Energies labeled 'sexual' represent only one small spectrum of the generative chakra energies. To channel all of your creative energies into sexual expressions and interactions would be to deny yourself the satisfaction of your own depth and breadth of creativity, and the world the contribution you can make above and beyond human reproduction.

To activate the generative chakra energies, ask yourself, "What do I want to *do,* what do I want to *bring into being* by my own creative activity, in this time/space of my life?" The range of choices is vast. You need not fear (or expect) that activation of these generative energies will lead to sexual activity and expression, for in consciousness you always have a choice of what to do and how to do it. You are not controlled by the arousal of sexual energies once you know that they are simply the slowest vibrations you register and transmit and that they can, on the breath-flow, simply be lifted to the frequency level of the *change you want to be* in any given situation.

The generative chakra energies represent the most basic, or fundamental, level of your personality-self expression. Without them, you could not move and have your being on this 'physical' plane of existence. Moreover, it is only when you give 'physical' expression to realities you create on other frequency levels of your being, that you become totally congruent and whole. To visualize a given reality in relation to something or someone, to want it, to pour out love for it, to think about it or talk about it, is not enough. When you *do* it, when you *become* it, your creative act is complete. The generative chakra represents that completion of the being and doing by the bringing of your creativity into expression in 'physical' or 'material' form.

The Solar Plexus

The solar plexus represents the energy frequencies we call feelings, or emotions. It corresponds to the area behind the navel, in the center of the back, and encompasses the digestive organs of the physical body.

On the frequencies of the solar plexus energies, you 'digest' your experiences as a personality and form responses to them which serve as motivations of your creative activities on the generative level. If you 'feel good' about a situation or person, you are able to act freely and respond fully on the 'physical' level, and you will want to make gifts of self and of creative self-expression. If you do not 'feel good,' you will be immobilized and have difficulty taking action, not wanting to give of self.

It is in the solar plexus that you create *problems* of your life-*opportunities*, for when you create hard feelings, develop irritation, resistance, resentment, you do not 'digest' the experiences. They stick in your throat, or are 'up-chucked' because they 'make you sick' and you are not able to process them in order to take from them life-giving energies of nourishment and learning.

You create *problems* for yourself when you refuse to bring into consciousness the feelings you register, or you refuse to express those feelings. In either case, you do not 'process' the experience and let it pass through your energy system.

To respond to a situation or person as an *opportunity,* all you have to do is to allow yourself to feel what you feel in order to free up your energies for action. Your *opportunity* lies in what you can be and do in response to your life situations and interactions. Allowing the feelings—whatever they are—to register in consciousness frees your motivating forces.

To activate your solar plexus energies, breathe deeply, filling your lungs entirely so that the diaphragm has an opportunity to expand fully. Totally relax all the muscles around and below your stomach. Breathe into the thoracic cavity. As you exhale, allow what you are feeling to surface into your awareness. 'Naming' what you feel will help you to identify it, because if you call it "anger" when it is actually "hurt," or "sympathy" when it is in fact "pity," you will experience a lack of resonance within your being. When you correctly identify it, you will experience the peace of self-understanding.

To give expression to feelings, or solar plexus energies, you can simply release them on the breath, or you can give voice to them in word or sound, or you can express them in some action (an embrace, a touch, the stomping of feet, the giving of a gift, doing an act of kindness, etc.) or in some other form of 'physical' release (a shiver, tears, laughter, trembling, etc.)

Only when you activate solar plexus energies, allowing yourself to be 'moved,' to feel, in response to life, will you be motivated to take action in your world and to give creative expression to your own life force. You will feel like living, have a zest for life, even if the feelings you are having, and are releasing, are painful or sad in some way. To feel is to 'touch' in your sensitivity the opportunity awaiting you in a given event in time/space, and to be able to respond to that opportunity.

The Heart Center

The heart center represents the balance point in the personality self. In it, the energies of the crown and sacral chakras unite to form a steady stream of connectedness to the Source—a flow of energy which we call universal love. The heart center corresponds to the center of the upper back, and encompasses the lungs and heart—in fact, your entire life-support system of breath and circulation.

Because the heart center energies represent a perfect balance between the negative and positive polarities of your autonomous field, they are energies which establish harmony in your own field as well as being very life-giving to others as they flow through you to them. To register heart center energies is to feel wholly and unconditionally loved and affirmed exactly as you are without your having to do anything to deserve or earn that love. It is to live in a state of grace.

For that reason, these energies can be activated in your consciousness by the application in your life of the **Love Project** principle *receive all people as beautiful exactly where they are,* starting with self.

To do this principle, and thus consciously activate heart center energies in your energy field, imagine that you have a hole in the top of your head through which you draw crown center energies down into your body, sending them on the breath-flow (as you inhale) down to the base of the spine (or to the soles of your feet if you are standing) where they contact the sacral chakra energies. Then lift them up to the heart center and breathe them out through imaginary nostrils in the center of your chest as you exhale. Then return your attention to the crown center as you inhale again, and continue the process so that you activate a continual flow of energy from the Source, through your own field, and out from you through the heart center.

153

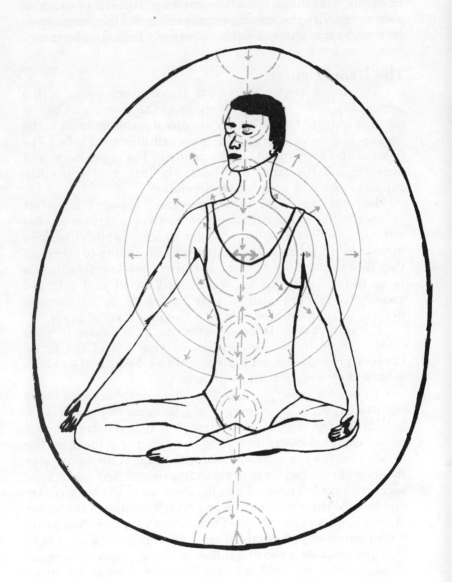

Each time you exhale through the heart center, imagine concentric circles of energy expanding outward in every direction. Feel the expansion of your own force-field and the exhilaration of that love force expressing through you, and imagine the love energy touching more and more people and blessing them with that life-giving power which is theirs to use in creative self-expression.

You can also practice reversing the flow, so that you start by drawing the life current up from the sacral center at the base of the spine to the crown center on the inhale, and then direct the energies down to the heart center to release them in an ever-expanding love energy as you exhale.

As you become more and more conscious of these energies, you will find joy increasing in your life. You will find you breathe more freely, move the energies of the other chakras with less difficulty, and have a growing sense of your intrinsic value, or worth, as an individualizing human being. You will be actively loving yourself, *receiving yourself as beautiful exactly where you are.* Notice that these energies do not require *thoughts or feelings* to change first, but only that you guide the flow of energy through your field with your conscious attention and awareness.

To activate heart center energies in relation to others, simply use those imaginary nostrils in the center of your chest both for the inhale and the exhale of the life force as it comes to you from other persons and flows from you to them. Receive all energy as it is into the heart center as love and sent it back with no conditions, no restrictions, no hesitations, no resistance, *no expectations.* To do so is to *receive all people as beautiful exaclty where they are,* for when you receive one person unconditionally, you open yourself to all others and free yourself to make the *choice* to receive them in the moment they enter your consciousness.

As you practice this activation of heart center energies, you will not only find your joy increasing hundredfold, but you will watch as all fear falls away. You will be able to be totally open, vulnerable and unafraid at all times under all circumstances, for you will never be caught or thrown off balance and you will be constantly replenishing your energy while sharing it with all persons with whom you come into contact.

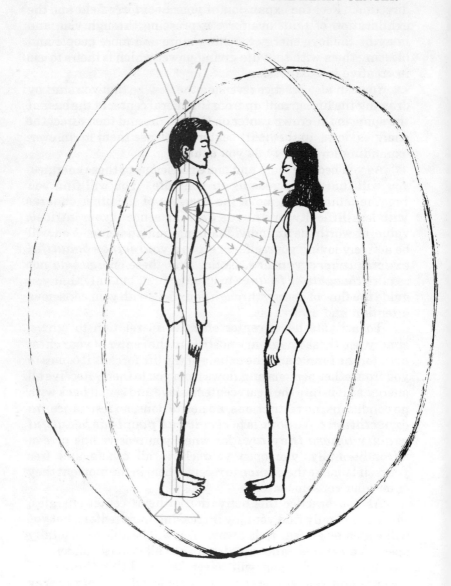

The Throat Chakra

It is on the energy frequencies of the throat chakra, which corresponds to the throat and embraces the vocal chords, that you register the fine lines of difference between the unending variety of facets and phases of the manifesting life force by giving them labels, or names. These labels, which we call words, enable you to consciously 'organize' your private energy world and, as your consciousness expands, the world around you. Throat chakra energies enable you to identify, categorize, analyze and file for future reference in your memory bank all data gathered from your life experience. On these energies you are able to transmit what you 'see' on the three eye center energies by forming them into thoughts and either writing or speaking them as a way of communicating with others.

Thus these energies enable you to *provide others with opportunities to give.* As you articulate your life experiences, you give other persons access to your private world, for the energies you transmit to them are ordered and identifiable on the frequencies of their own throat chakra energies.

To activate the throat center energy frequencies consciously, write about your daily experiences, describing them as fully as you can. Include dream experiences in your daily log. Also, write to and for other persons. Write letters. Write short stories. Share your writings with friends.

Reading what others have written, or listening to them talk, will also help. Take courses which require you to entertain new thoughts and mental disciplines. Analyze and evaluate the writings and discourses of others, making sense out of them in your own private world.

Finally, practice back-and-forth communication with other persons in dialogues or discussions of various kinds. Make your self-expression through the medium of words as clear and orderly as you possibly can.

As you learn to register these frequencies in greater and greater consciousness, you will find yourself feeling more and more self-confident, more and more in charge of, in control of, your self, your private world, your creative expression on all levels.

Simultaneously, you will be able to take in more and more from other persons without experiencing confusion, a loss of self-control, or a dissipation of your energies. You will find yourself feeling so much stronger as a person that you will be able to manifest your gentleness, openness and even needfulness with ever-increasing ease, maintaining a clearheadedness all the while that will sustain your sense of self-control even in the most difficult of situations.

The Three Eyes or 'Seeing' Center

What is often called the third eye center is three wavebands of energy frequencies combined into one—all having to do with 'seeing.' The 'first eye' registers the energy frequencies corresponding to the generative chakra, enabling us to 'see' what we call 'physical' objects. The 'second eye' registers the energy frequencies corresponding to the solar plexus, heart and throat center energies, enabling us to 'see' what we call feelings and thoughts and the forms they take—what are often called 'psychic' or 'etheric' energies.

The 'third eye' enables us to 'see' the energy frequencies corresponding to autonomous fields—those energy patterns that are determinative on the personality level in the human being and that characterize the interplay between positive and negative polarities on all levels of being in manifestation.

It is on the three eyes frequencies that you become *conscious of the reality you have created* for yourself. *You create the reality*—bring it into being—on all of the energy frequencies corresponding to the personality self. However, only on the frequencies of the three eyes center do you 'see' what you have created, bring it into your awareness, and thus become able to *take conscious charge of it.* These frequencies are the link between the unconscious, or 'automatic,' functioning of the lower (slower) vibrations of the first four personality-self chakras—the generative, solar plexus, heart and throat centers—and those energy frequencies which correspond to the autonomous field itself, namely the crown and sacral chakra forces.

To activate the energy frequencies of the 'seeing' center, practice conscious awareness of all you register in the other six centers of your being. Watch yourself in the midst of your living. Adopt the stance of an observer. The more conscious you become, the more you see yourself and the world as you/it are, the more fully you will be able to activate your Higher Self and make free *choices.*

Practice distinguishing between what you do (generative chakra), feel (solar plexus), think (throat chakra) and 'see' (third-eye chakra), for your actions, feelings and thoughts constitute the *reality* you have brought into being and live within. You can only make new *choices* under the guidance of Higher Self about the *reality you register/create* when you are *conscious* of what it is, and can 'see' what direction to go. That consciousness is a function of the three eyes, or 'seeing' center.

Each person is an individualizing expression of the universal life force, or God, functioning very much like an electrical adaptor. The life force flows into you and out of you, and you have ability to adapt the current as you wish, increasing or decreasing the life charge you transmit. As you expand your consciousness, you increase your capacity to transmit more and more power. The lines of force with which you will be connected will increase in number. The more conscious you are, the more central you become to the larger energy web of which you are a part, for the charge of universal force passing through you increases the amperage available to a widening circle of conscious beings within the sphere of your contact. You will become an ever more powerful channel of energy, touching a multitude of 'others' with love as you shine with the light of understanding and knowledge, your heart center singing with joy.*

---

*For further reading on the chakras read *The Psychology of Enlightenment: Meditations on the Seven Energy Centers,* by Gurudev Shree Chitrabhanu, Dodd, Mead & Company, 1979, and *Joy's Way: A Map for the Transformational Journey,* by W. Brugh Joy, M.D., J.P. Tarcher, Inc., 1978.

Chapter Nine
THE PRINCIPLES
IN CONCERT

In order to be fully loving, to live in total harmony with self and others, we must activate all the **Love Project** principles at once. Until now, we have been focusing on each principle separately, getting on the inside of how each one can be made to work in your life. As the last chapter clearly revealed, however, each of the principles corresponds to only one of the wave-bands of energy frequencies in which we function. When we are in perfect balance, therefore, all of the energy centers are open and we are doing all of the principles fully all at once. Our whole being is 'in concert,' functioning in total harmony.

The principles, therefore, though stated as six separate guidelines for living, are actually all needed to make a complete statement of love with your life. To return to our earlier definition of love as unblocked life energy flowing through your being, we can now see that there are seven different wave-bands of life energy to activate and to keep flowing freely. The principles are one way of bringing those seven bands of energy into our consciousness so that we can cooperate with the process of unblocked energy flow which is the natural state of our being.

The more we expand our consciousness of our own process of living, the more of the energy frequencies represented by the seven chakras we are able to release in the course of our everyday living. Likewise, the more we practice being and doing the six **Love Project** principles, the more depth and breadth of application we discover in them. Practicing each of the principles individually enables us to do all of them in concert with greater and greater ease.

By the same token, to practice one of the principles while ignoring another can be self-defeating. For example, to *perceive a problem as an opportunity* is wonderful. However, if you then harbor secret *expectations* about *what* the *opportunity* is going to be, you may create still another *problem.* The *expectation* may not materialize, and you may find yourself disappointed or frustrated. Or, your *expectation* may come into being, limiting what was your *opportunity* and barring you from realizing your full potential in that situation.

Or, if you decide to *be the change you want to see happen* with the *expectation* that *that* will change your partner when nothing else has worked, you will have unblocked energy in one center only to block it again in another.

Or, if you try to convince someone else to *receive* a third party *as beautiful exactly where he/she is,* you may find that person resents *you* for not simply *being the change you want to see happen* by *receiving both parties as beautiful exactly where they are,* instead of trying to change one or the other.

If you become enamored of your proficiency in executing one of the principles, you may discover that you are doing it at the expense of another, thereby creating imbalance instead of harmony. For example, over-activity in the three eyes center may render you a master at *creating your own reality consciously,* but you may neglect to activate the throat chakra, rarely *providing others with the opportunity to give to you.* Consequently, you may wake up one day to find yourself trapped even more totally in your private world, conscious though you may be that you created it. Your single-minded focus on *creating your own reality consciously* may cause you to loose perspective on your personal reality as only one of myriad realities. In addition, you might find yourself dealing with the *problem* of loneliness as a result of having neglected your feelings and needs as they gathered in your solar plexus, so centered were you in your reflective mind.

Or, you may learn to *receive yourself and all others as beautiful right where they are* but neglect to activate your own creative energy in *being the change you want to see happen* in the world and thus fail to make your own creative contribution and your unique impact on the group psyche. Settling totally into *receiving* may result in total passivity and even inactivity instead of liberating you from blinding judgment and crippling feelings *in order* that you might be fully, actively, uninhibitedly who *you* are.

While practicing all the principles simultaneously does require consciousness, it is not as difficult as it might seem on the surface. To the contrary. The principles actually facilitate one another, for it is the natural life process to function evenly through all seven chakras. The process is hampered only when *you* get in the way of what is proceeding in natural order. You would be doing the **Love Project** principles without thinking, as easily as breathing or walking, if you were not in some way blocking your natural flow. Observing your life process in the midst of living will enable you to become cognizant of how you are actually being and doing the principles most of the time. To come to know that without effort you *are* practicing them is to aid you in activating them at will, in taking command of your life when you create blocks that temporarily throw you out of balance.

This chapter is devoted to examples from real life situations, shared by **Seekers** who have been consciously practicing the **Love Project** principles in their lives for a number of years now, and who have experienced the transforming power of unblocked energy, or love. You will see how the activation of all of the principles enabled these persons to engage in life situations productively, harmoniously, growthfully and joyfully, bringing enrichment to themselves and to others whose lives they touched.

As you read along, we encourage you to begin to examine actual life situations of your own in which you are currently involved, or in which you engaged in the past, to see how all of the principles are, could be, or indeed were activated. If you want to live in a pool of love, you might as well dive right in and learn all the strokes at once so that you can enjoy your new life to the fullest and discover the truly re-creational benefits of exercising love-muscles.

A Time of Confrontation

My friend Arleen and I had been enthusiastically related for over a year to an artist-poet friend whom I shall call Ben. We were so excited about his creational works that we had offered ourselves to be the channels through which his works might be published and thus released to a larger audience. We signed a "Love Agreement" with Ben, agreeing that he would provide the works and we would do the publishing as our mutual expressions of service to the One rather than as any ordinary business contract through which both parties hoped to 'make money.'

As time went on, however, Arleen and I discovered that our commitments to our work in **The Love Project** simply did not enable us, time and energy-wise, to get to the publishing of Ben's works. Moreover, money had not been made available to us to do the works, and we felt that to be an indication, along with other things too numerous to mention here, that it was no longer in harmony with the 'big picture' for us to carry through with the plans we had originally made. Therefore we wrote to Ben, asking to be released from our Love Agreement in order that both he and we be free to get on with our respective work in service to the One. Ben, after a considerable silence, said that he felt this was too important a decision to be made by mail or telephone, and asked that we come to see him.

Having no hidden agenda myself, I approached the day of our meeting with Ben with absolutely *no expectations*. Instead, I was totally confident that all would work out according to the larger will, and in total trust and *abundant expectancy*, I looked forward to this time of sharing with our good friend.

When we arrived at Ben's on the day of our appointed meeting, I was *consciously creating the reality* of joy and total openness. I embraced Ben and the friend he was chatting with as we entered, expressing my delight to be with Ben again and to make the acquaintance of his friend. The friend, whom we shall call Phil, then said, "I wish it were on a happier occasion that we were meeting. I am Ben's lawyer and am here to serve you with a summons. We are suing you for breach of contract and for $30,000 in damages."

Because I had had *no expectations* and was *receiving myself and Ben and his friend as beautiful exactly where we all were,* this announcement, which took me totally by surprise, did not throw me off balance. And because I had been *consciously creating the reality* of openness, I had no difficulty receiving it, and perceiving it, as an

163

opportunity rather than a problem. I registered his words in my consciousness, received a blow to the solar plexus and immediately absorbed the impact of it, releasing the energy. I had been in court only once in my life. I had not liked the experience, and in my feeling self I registered a momentary rush of fear at the thought of going to court again. Then I breathed deeply, let go of the fear, and felt instead the calm associated with the total trust of *abundant expectancy.*

My observer self was fully active, watching my process and the other persons in the room as well. It seemed to me that Phil, the lawyer, was functioning primarily in solar plexus and throat chakras energies, while Ben seemed to be almost entirely centered in his solar plexus frequencies. I made the *conscious choice* to channel my energies through the heart center, consciously *receiving* both of them as *beautiful exactly where they were* while *being the change I wanted to see happen* in that situation.

Through the throat chakra, Arleen and I both began to *provide Ben with opportunities to give to us* by sharing our processes and inviting him to do the same if he would like. The *change I wanted to see happen* was that we *not* take this matter to court but rather settle it together like the loving friends we were. I wanted, therefore, to establish bridges of trust and communication, and I set about doing that from my side by trusting both Ben and Phil to be true to their own inner beings and by seeking to understand what had brought them to feel they wanted to, or had to, file a suit against us.

I shared my own thoughts and feelings in order to invite them into my process, and kept leaving the door to my inner being open, *receiving them* in *as beautiful*, and affirming them for staying true to their own processes.

After two hours Phil left us, expressing his confidence that we would work things out between ourselves. He embraced us, saying that he thought he understood where we were coming from.

For another hour, Ben, Arleen and I worked together to find a common ground of understanding upon which we could stand to work out a plan of action which would enable us all to *be the change we wanted to see happen.*

By the end of a month, we had straightened everything out to all of our satisfaction, and Ben withdrew his suit. He reaffirmed his friendship with us and his trust of us, and to this day the love energy continues to flow between us. Meanwhile, I learned a great deal about not making commitments that I was not certain I could carry through, and about not stating as a reality (in this case, that the money would be there to publish the works) that which I know in the crown chakra but have yet to manifest through the generative chakra, for such mixing of levels can be very confusing to others. I was grateful for the experience throughout, cooperating with our friend Ben rather than getting caught up in fear and worry and struggle, which could have blocked the life energy flow that kept us bound together in love.

Diane K. Pike
San Diego, CA

A Time of Neighborly Sharing

I was out in the garden weeding, certainly with no thought at all that this was to be an eventful, let alone monumental, day. Suddenly my attention was drawn to the sound of sobbing just over the fence behind the bush in my neighbor's yard. I moved instinctively toward the tears. My re-mind interrupted, saying, "Perhaps you should mind your own business." I registered the thought, and let it go. I reasoned that if I were weeping in pain and another human being was nearby and possibly capable of helping me, I would at least want the offer. I would want the option of receiving or rejecting the help. if it were not offered, I would not have that choice.

This process of inner examination led me to *be the change I wanted to see happen* in that moment. I stepped forward to find my neighbor slumped over on an old wooden bench, wiping her eyes with her apron. Gently I asked if I could be of help.

I had extended my energy freely, with no strings attached. I wanted her to feel free to share with me or not to share. I didn't wish to intrude, but I was *providing her with the opportunity to give to me,* to share some of the burden she was carrying, in order that I might give to her in return. I waited.

She acknowledged my presence and my offer with a slight lift of her head. I could almost see her deciding whether or not to speak. Then she turned toward me and blurted out through increased sobbing that her oldest son had had a severe stroke, was paralyzed on one side, had double vision, and worst of all, had given up hope. She wished it had happened to her and not to him.

For the next half hour I talked with her—gently, lovingly. I encouraged her to cry, to let her feelings flow. I made whatever suggestions I could to help facilitate the family's process in this crisis. We gave to each other and received from each other.

I could feel energy rising in me. I saw so many possibilities, innumerable things that both she and her son could do. Yet, I knew that I could not do those things for them. Nor could I change the way they viewed the event. They refused to see any *opportunities* in the *problem;* they were still too deeply involved in regret and sadness.

I breathed deeply, *receiving them both as beautiful exactly where they were.* I was not there to live their lives for them—only to love them and help as best I could. I could only offer; what they chose to receive was up to them.

The energy continued to rise in me. I felt her pain, and yet I was filled with exultation. From the depth of my own personal crisis experiences I knew intimately the joy of *problems being opportunities.* My thoughts rattled on like an endless series of box cars filled with "if only's." If only he could lift himself above the effects of the stroke and see the whole picture from his Higher Self. If only he knew he could choose to see the opportunities. If only he knew he had the power to set healing energy in motion. If only.....if only. I thought I would explode.

Then, right there in the garden, a voice spoke to me with great force. "You will write a book called 'Why Me?' It will be a handbook for the stricken. It will be for all those persons who are asking, 'Why Me?' and who need to know that only they can answer the question. You will write it as the echo of their own Higher Selves so that they can take themselves by the hand and guide themselves through the healing process."

I stood flabbergasted. I knew a great deal about healing, but surely not enough to fill a book. I wasn't an 'authority.' I wasn't even sure what I would say. Yet, I said, "Yes." I make it a practice not to say "No" to the Universe when it speaks to me, when it asks something of me. I was not about to *create the reality* that only persons with medical degrees or faith ordinations could speak on this subject. Instead, I *consciously affirmed a reality I had long ago created,* that all of us know all we need to know about everything. All knowledge and wisdom is recorded within the consciousness of every cell of every being. It awaits our awakening to it. It is not that we learn it having never known it; rather, we remind ourselves of what we already know by calling it into our awareness.

Having fully *created that reality* for myself, I lovingly took leave of my neighbor, who was wanting to be alone just then, and headed for the house with such determination that I felt as if a finger were pushing at my back. My neighbor's *problem had become my opportunity* to make an important contribution to her, to her son, perhaps to the world.

I walked through the kitchen, announcing to Diane that I was going to write a book called "Why Me?", and sat down immediately with pencil and paper. I had no idea what I would write; nor did I have any *expectations*. I was filled instead with *abundant expectancy*, knowing that what needed to emerge would. This was, after all, a collaboration with the Universe. Looking deep within my inner wisdom, I said silently, "I'm ready. Let's begin."

Each step along the way I made no demands on myself. I simply *received myself as beautiful exactly where I was,* not laboring over anything, being patient, allowing the chapters to take shape with *abundant expectancy*. I knew that people guide themselves through any dis-ease once they choose to. By giving birth to this book I could *be the change I wanted to see happen* in relation to healing without attempting to change anyone else. I kept writing, delighting in what was emerging.

Two weeks later (!) the initial manuscript was completed. It was amazing—an incredible experience of allowing wisdom to flow through me.

Now it is out there in the world, in bookstores, in people's hands—an available aid, in the form of a book, to those who are ready to move *beyond their problems to the opportunities* within them.

The **Love Project** principles facilitated the birth of *Why Me? How to Heal What's Hurting You.** They helped me to rise above questions of myself which might have convinced me that I was not capable of such an endeavor. They helped me to make a contribution to myself, to my neighbor, to the human family. They served me by keeping my energy flowing, by allowing something larger than my thoughts to flow through me.

Arleen Lorrance
San Diego, CA

The Death of a Loved One

Many experiences occur during our lives. It is not necessarily the experience that is frightening or devastating but the way in which we handle it. *Choice is the life process,* and we can guide our thinking and subsequent actions, allowing the *energy* to *flow* instead of short-circuiting it.

As a result of learning and living the **Love Project** principles, I've found myself constantly growing in my ability to cope with life. To me life is a classroom of experiences to be discovered, worked with, and understood 'till we begin to realize what could be another **Love Project** principle— "Everything's O.K."

Usually, if we grow a lot, it's from a particularly big problem, for *problems are opportunities.*

Five years ago, my wife, who had been extremely healthy, developed (through a chain of circumstances) terminal cancer. Fortunately, I believe that we are all 'spirit' (energy), and that life is just temporarily personified in the form of a particular 'person,' and that 'death' is just a moving forward to another classroom of experiences. My belief was to be put to the test when, nearly three years ago, my wife died.

What were my thoughts, feelings and plans when after nearly 30 years of marriage, I was alone? I had many varied feelings. I felt appreciation that God had chosen to call her home when He/She did, so that she did not linger on, suffering. I felt a deep void, for particularly in the last months as she had of necessity come to depend on me physically more and more,

---

*Rawson Associates, 1978

we'd become closer than ever before. Now she was 'gone.' I cried many tears, those that I could not shed in front of her and those that I felt for the future lifetime we would miss having together. A particular love song on the radio would start me off, or a phone call from someone who hadn't heard, or uncanceled mail subscriptions in her name.

As I let the tears flood out, I was aware that I was crying for myself—my loneliness, my hurt. Deep inside of me I was grateful that she was no longer suffering, and I knew "All is well for her now" and that she'd moved toward a higher plateau of growth.

We have innumerable choices. Thus I looked at myself as an 'observer,' and viewed the many alternatives open to me. I could keep crying, pull myself (through running down my health) into a disease. I could stand in the corner and pout, damning life with a "Why me?" attitude. *Create your own reality* and *be the change you want to see happen* were principles that stuck out in my mind. Don't spend weeks on 'mind trips' of "What if's," I told myself. Just do it.

So it was that, just a few weeks after I'd buried my wife, I decided to be the person I want to be: happy, loving, caring and sharing, starting from "just where I was." I began a merry-go-round of meetings for personal growth, self-discovery and religion to discover that all paths lead to the same God, and that we are all ONE. There is unity in the diversity of life. With this discovery I was able finally to understand how to *receive all persons as beautiful exactly where they are,* a principle I'd struggled with for years.

New doors opened, strangers became friends, a new life emerged. I found that I could be alone, and whereas it is nice to have friends, I no longer *had* to have them. I could survive with or without them.

The mysteries of life started to unfold for me and a new awesome and exciting world of understanding began to make life more and more worthwhile for me. I give thanks for the blessings I have, appreciating the smiling grace of God which reminds me of the truth of who I really am, and as the fog clears I see more and more until on a clear day I can see forever.

Ron Podrow
San Diego, CA

My Recovery from a Suicide Attempt

Looking back can be worthwhile when the flashback pictures of yourself begin with you at the bottom of the pit and then continue on with your steady ascent up a spiral stairway of self-knowledge, spiritual insight, and growth.

I was recovering from a deep depression culminating from the break-up of a thirty-one-year marriage, continuing remorse over a son whose sociopathic behavior necessitated his imprisonment, and chronic sciatic pain that had worsened with the added stress of teaching a 3rd/4th grade class over-burdened with emotionally disturbed children. I had felt that I was no longer needed by anyone, that I had nothing worthwhile to offer life here.

Five months from the day I decided to end my life (the Father let me go that far before He sent in the rescue team), I met the two influential people who showed me the easiest way to climb my Jacob's ladder, via the **Love Project** principles.

With that first **Love Project** weekend's introduction to how to channel my love energy I began putting back together the larger pieces of my life. I was reminded that the first piece in the new picture puzzle of Millie had to be me. And I learned from the very loving, supportive group of **Seekers** that until I could *receive myself as beautiful where I was* in my evolvement I would continue to lack self-confidence in the love and talents I had to give to my world.

I began to see that I *could make choices* and **create a whole new reality** out of the rest of my life on this plane.

The situation of the overly-sick class that had defeated eight substitute teachers following my exit, alerted the school staff to a problem that *provided them with the opportunity to give* by dividing the class and parceling out the emotionally disturbed children to three or four teachers instead of overloading one. My problem had been a gift to them by showing them *their* problem. I had also given the school administration the *opportunity to give* me the gift of trusting me with another class.

The relationship with my son took a new turning as I rid myself of the last remnants of self-blame, and let go of the responsibility I had still carried for his sad development, and saw both of us as *beautiful right where we were.* I could now write those weekly letters without smearing the ink with my tears of "if only's," sending instead messages of love and support *having no expectations* as to what he would do with his life, but rather *abundant expectancy* that he will fulfill his destiny as he chooses, either in this lifetime or another.

By *being the change I wanted to see happen instead of trying to change everyone else,* I found I could *receive my former husband as beautiful right where he was* in exploring his new lifestyle, *giving up expectations* that we could salvage our marriage, but rather having *abundant expectancy* that I could *create a new and beautiful life in reality by consciously controlling,* with the guidance of my Higher Self, *those choices I make.* This traumatic separation from my husband was in truth a *gift he had given me,* a gift that held *opportunities* for growth and development I had failed to explore in my former dependent, wifely role.

I, in turn, because *I see him as beautiful right where he is,* have chosen to give him my loving support as he, too, searches for his path in his pattern of life. Consequently, we both enjoy the gift of a fine relationship with love flowing freely between us.

I have chosen to make peace with my physical pain which is perhaps the Universe's reminder to be more loving of this body I chose to live in that took on the physical weaknesses of both earthly parents (by my consent.) Then, too, I look to my frequent bouts of physical discomfort as the gift that has made me more compassionate of the suffering of others.

Twinges and aches are a very minor concern in my life now as *I live for the change I want to see happen*, and that is to look for the good and the beautiful in all things and let love rule my life...unconditional love.

Millie Boucher
La Jolla, CA

Living with a Physical Handicap

During the years in which I was growing and taking shape, putting roots into the soil of my life, I had many aspirations, hopes and desires, plus a fair amount of creative disturbance and restlessness. I lacked self-confidence and was apt to put faith in people around me and other external realities rather than in myself. It took many experiences to reach a point of knowing that almost everything was motivated from inside me, not from outside, and all that was unconsciousness. Somehow during this seminal period, especially the early part, I saw time as a rubber band that I could stretch without limits. There was always tomorrow or some distant point in the future. Fortunately for me, I found a number of fertile gardens along the way so that I was able to eat of the fruits of wholeness and awareness. One of those fruits was **The Love Project** and its principles.

Recently, a deteriorating heart condition caused my time-stretching rubber band to snap back and bring to the fore the burning question of whether I would have many more tomorrows. However, I had by this stage of my growth integrated the **Love Project** principles into my soul. More often than not I lived the principles simultaneously, in their entirety, in the full flow of their totality during each day. I had *become the change I wanted to see happen.*

In the case of my body's illness, I chose to consciously participate, with the help of the plenteous energies of my quintessance, in my own healing. My body had served me well throughout my years, even when I had disregarded its needs. I recognized in some way that I had chosen this form of disruption or disease in order to bring my consciousness to another level. I began to re-evaluate my priorities. I let go of those activities that seemed unimportant to the real nature of life and of my being.

What could have been a *problem* became an *opportunity* to change. I realized I could no longer live my yesterdays or have *expectations* about tomorrow. Being here in this moment, living it as fully as possible, became a way of life. I've taught myself to be sensitive to the *abundant expectancy* of the moment and *not to have expectations.* For me this means, to see and hear; to be open to the sounds of the now, the ticking clock, the chirping bird, the din of traffic, children playing, the full music of life. The entire sensation I have is of a vibrant, pulsating, living organism here, now, alive in this precious moment.

At times, because of habit, I unconsciously do something in my old way. I lift an object or walk at my old pace or do some activity in the manner I had been accustomed to, and my body sends out an immediate message. I have a *choice;* I can ignore the message. I can take it as a crippling blow, full of despair. Or I can love my body for its direction, for its care, and *receive it as beautiful exactly as it is.* Most of the time I receive it as a gift that is beautiful. It has been a learning and as I continue to improve and grow in loving myself, I have been able to *receive more and more people as beautiful exactly where they are.* I find that what seemed like imperfections in myself and others were only my *expectations* of how we should have been.

Finding myself physically unable to do what I once did without thought or concern caused me to seek remedial assistance. I let go of old fears, distrust and discomfort with the medical profession. I sought out and responded with openness to a number of physicians and their subsequent tests. I *provided them with the opportunity to give to me* in the mode they knew best. Many of them were not only efficient in their medical demeanor but were warm, considerate and caring people.

I also needed to let go of old social graces, patterns or attitudes I had lived by. This required a depth of humility I had not often experienced; I was not in charge, and even more, I had to ask for help. I had to be open to receive and once again *provide others with the opportunity to give.* This was evident in heretofore little thought of matters like carrying groceries from the market, taking out trash, helping to clean the house and car, or other expected behavior in the everyday, working world. It was not easy, especially at first, but as time moved on I became aware I had the power within me to re-define myself, to re-create myself at every level of consciousness.

To create my own reality is to include and live all the principles at once in any given experience. I am not whole or flowing if I compartmentalize myself or the principles. They are intrinsically bound to each other, as are chakra centers, as are all life processes. *Creating my own reality consciously rather than living as if I had no control over my life* seems to be the end point; to view the universe through love. More and more I am able to do this, able to be in the present moment. To be love and to be truth, the ancient truth of the spirit, is to experience God as the ultimate and greatest

173

meaning. It is through these patterns, these energies, that all disease, all pain, all the wornout bodies and spent selves will be renewed and transformed.

Sid Stave
Ukiah, CA

Living Love in a Marriage

With almost all our peers having affairs and/or getting divorced, we feel like a minority as we approach our sixteenth wedding anniversary, and we use all the emotional and spiritual helps we can. Out of therapy and growth group experiences, we came to believe we could *grow* through this life situation—marriage and family life—rather than surviving it with standard escapes and aids such as alcohol, tranquilizers, eighty-hour work weeks, etc.

Some of the tools we use are the **Love Project** principles and practice sessions with Diane and Arleen and other **Seekers**. As a matter of fact, they deserve some of the credit for our making it through the past several years of accelerated growth and change.

Some people of our generation may identify with the generalities of our situation. We were married right after my graduation from college. David had graduated six months earlier and left for Naval flight training. I had been raised on Doris Day movies and fairy tales with princes, so I *expected* David to fill the bill and ensure that I live happily ever after. David had been relatively wild and uncontrolled. He was looking for someone weak and childlike emotionally; I *expected* him to be strong, controlled and rational. We set out to play the masculine and feminine roles, which fit perfectly with our personalities, and we established a relationship based on the masculine and feminine cultural stereotypes.

We were not self-actualized, whole persons coming to the relationship. We both had remained dependent on our parents, and we traded in our parents for each other, *expecting* the other to be what we needed. As we are moving toward becoming whole and complete—incorporating those qualities into ourselves which we had been attracted to in our mate—the individual changes are causing changes in the marriage relationship. We are now trying to find the balance between an

174

independent sense of self within a relationship and the mutuality of becoming fully human together—not totally dependent or independent, but interdependent.

We took Diane and Arleen's request for an article as an *opportunity.* The request came in the midst of one more revision of our relationship from changes in one member of the relationship. The real challenge is to break down the old roles, stereotypes, cultural and family programing without breaking up the relationship. At times it seems easier to 'bail out,' thinking we would leave the old patterns behind. We know that even if it were that easy to leave the negative behind, we would also be leaving a lot of positive behind. We were struck with the chance to affirm our commitment to this sixteen-year relationship with a new set of marriage vows, vows patterned after the **Love Project** principles and an expression of the man and woman we are today.

Hers

I, Anne, see life as an *opportunity* to grow as a human, a physical, emotional, mental/intellectual and spiritual being and a woman. I see my shared life with David as enhancing that process of growth for both of us because of the commitment, the potential for intimacy and the possibility for unity in diversity.

I will *be the change instead of trying to change David.* I will be myself, express myself—all my feelings regardless of how parts of myself or David label them or fear them. I'll be open, loving and vulnerable. I will put my energy into working on my own stuff instead of on David's stuff. I will keep my communication current and congruent. I will be my highest and best for my own sake and the sake of the universe, not to please my mate or to keep him.

I will *receive myself and David as beautiful exactly where we are.* I know that we are independent persons who carry unique backgrounds, traits, needs and styles into this moment. I know that we came here as individual souls, and are beautiful.

I will relate adult to adult and *provide opportunities to give* by stating my needs. I will no longer act as a child to get my needs met, or play parent/rescuer to meet David's needs. I can nurture and be nurtured, but do it consciously and not in the old games or patterns. I will take responsibility for all my needs (including sexual), behavior, circumstances, and not play victim of personalities or situations.

I will perceive any **problems as opportunities** to grow and expand. I know they are not only opportunities for the individuals but also for the relationship to reach new levels of growth, expansion, awareness and consciousness.

I will **have no expectations** of my self, David, or the relationship. I will have **abundant expectancy** that if I can let go of the old, and do not try to create the new from the old, the new will be better than any of my expectations. I am willing to experience the void as I let go of old forms and give up my need to create a new form, allowing it to emerge in its own time, space and form.

I will **create my own reality consciously**. I choose to fulfill my own potential so that I can come to the relationship as a whole person. I know I have a need to relate, and I will consciously choose as an individual, married to an individual, committed to a relationship. I will not be swept along by unconscious choices, mass consciousness, archetypes about marriage, recordings, cultural trends, etc. I **create my own realities** regardless of anything else going on anywhere.

His

Dear Anne:

This is not a "Dear John" letter, dear Anne—for I am deeply committed to our marriage and to the bond of loving and caring we have built for over sixteen years.

The **Love Project** principles allow me to see where I've mismanaged my life in the past. They also help me turn my commitment into positive action.

I now choose to **create the reality of our marriage relationship consciously**. In the past my behavior has been dominated by patterns that I accepted without question and followed without conscious evaluation. I did what I believed society, my parents and my peers expected me to do. I am now aware of most of those patterns and I will use my own inner wisdom to evaluate and consciously choose those actions that seem congruent and valuable to me.

I will *have no expectations.* Since I worked hard to fulfill what I perceived to be the expectations of society, parents and peers—I was a "good" father, son and husband—I expected results. I expected to be loved, accepted and happy. When all my expectations were not met I was frustrated, resentful and angry. I still find it difficult to break the old patterns and give up the expectations. I will, however, begin now to love and trust my inner self, to allow my actions to flow from my center and *then* to have *abundant expectancy—* knowing that activity thus generated can only have positive results.

Some of those results will be marvelous opportunities for growth. I am determined to *receive difficult times as opportunities, not problems.* I know that all the difficulties generated by our relationship are really windows to my soul—a perfect opportunity for me to look deep within myself, to learn and to grow.

I earnestly desire to *be the change I want to see happen.* I have long operated on the incorrect assumption that 'our relationship' was a tangible entity, something I could "work on." I now recognize four facets of our marriage: the individual-you, the individual-me, your perception of our relationship, and my perception of our relationship. I can only change, or "work on," two of the four facets—I cannot control you or your perceptions.

In the past I have tried to control you. You were not meeting my expectations. I expected you to know what I wanted—but if you didn't come through, I knew how to manipulate you. (For example, I knew withdrawal frightened you—so I could get angry, withdraw, frighten you, and you would shape up.) When you learned to break the manipulation game it frustrated a very old pattern.

You are a growing, changing person—and I can *receive you as beautiful exactly where you are.* When I want something from you, I will do this *without expectations, knowing* that your response will always be perfect for me and perfect for you.

Daily, hourly, *I make the choices* that create my life

situation. I choose to live and be and grow with you.

Anne McLaren,
David McLaren
Newport Beach, CA

Learning to Love My Self

I'd been emerging from a lifestyle of shyness and social awkwardness. I had worked on myself for years and had made great strides, a lot of which had to do with being comfortable with other people. I was now finding myself being "popular." I was in seventh heaven and saw no reason for it to end. Then it seemed like all at once a major part of my support system fell away. Friends moved away and a girl I was very much attached to and loved, left. It felt like I was falling apart; I was hurt and angry with myself and the world. After all, I had worked so hard for so many years to create what I was now labeling a support system outside myself. I couldn't believe so much of my support centered outside myself, but I kept reliving and reminding myself of the pain and hurt so I continually experienced myself without support and in pain. I was *creating a reality* for myself that fed upon itself to create even more pain. What I was doing was beating myself up and blaming it on something outside of me.

For months all I did was relive the pain and hurts, crying all the way. I wasn't about to really do anything for myself because it all fell away anyway, so what was the point in trying?

During that time, I was attending group therapy sessions. At one point the therapist and I had a big blow-up with each other. It felt like I had nobody on my side, not even me.

Then one night as I was driving around crying, I realized that if I wanted to stop hurting I was going to have to do something for me.

Shortly after that, I made a *choice* to start doing some body work. I joined a health studio and started lifting weights, finishing each session with a jacuzzi. I added some yoga exercises, and within a couple of weeks I started loosening up enough to feel and sometimes even think of something else besides my constant pain and self-harrassment. I started to *be the change I wanted to see happen* by doing more things that I thought might feel good.

Now, I didn't know if what I chose to do would work or not. I had *no expectations* but only *abundant expectancy*, for my experience told me that 'things' don't work, they fall away instead. But I was still around, I was left with me and now I was starting to work for me.

I began to see and experience that me working for me was just the help I needed. I was *providing myself with the opportunity to give to me* and was actively cashing in on it. I was also *receiving myself as beautiful right where I was* by owning all parts of myself and acknowledging the intent of each part to help me in some way. After a while it became a simple matter of organizing myself to match the intent.

For example, when I was asked to write this paper as something that might be in a book, I was flattered. When I started writing this "important" paper, however, I started beating on myself because I wanted it to be perfect. I would take a break and treat myself to something that felt good. After a few times of doing this—beating and treating—I decided to *provide myself with the opportunity* to do this paper in a way that I didn't have to beat myself to get it done. As the deadline drew near and I still didn't have it done, I actively gave myself many gifts of appreciation, *received myself as beautiful right where I was,* and decided that this was so whether I got the paper done or not.

For me it became clear that I was the one who was "important." After that the paper became fun to write. This was really neat for me because it's the so-called "important" things that I trip on. Organizing my experiences, as I receive them with the resources I need to handle them, in a way that is comfortable and promotes growth, is one way I *create my reality consciously.* This keeps me in charge of organizing my experiences and not the experiences organizing me.

I learn a lot by *problems being opportunities.* Like how to give to myself gifts that help, to handle the 'problems,' to grow and to do so with increasing joy and comfort.

Carl Downing
San Marcos, CA

Retirement,
Or How to Create a
New Reality Consciously

I'd watched many people reach the retirement time in their lives and just stop living, vegetate and die. They were folks with lots of potential still untapped who might have gone on contributing joyfully to life. I wanted none of that for me.

As time approached for me to retire from a lively and varied teaching and counseling career, I realized several facts about me and my way of relating. One was that my enjoyment of people would still continue and that I needed to be in contact with people. Another was that I was still active and full of energy. Still another was that I wanted, as well as needed, to work in order to keep alert, meet people and have enough income to continue to live as I was accustomed. I was *receiving myself as beautiful exactly where I was.* O.K. then, what to do?

Consider *problems as opportunities* for growth, for giving or receiving, for flowing with universal energy, for being open to inspiration. They are presented to help us look at ourselves and then move towards actively solving them.

Action for me was imagining myself in all sorts of new activities, *not* related to my former occupations. I thought of leadership roles in recreation, in church activities, in senior citizen activities. But these were all related to past experiences. What were some other interests in my life? As I pondered, it came to me. Books, Books, Books!! I love them, always have, and expect to forever. I like to see them on shelves in people's homes and to keep myself surrounded with them. I like to handle them and I'd been a reader all my life.

There was, at that time, a large new shopping mall under construction in my rapidly growing community. I checked out what stores were leasing and found that a large chain was to open a bookstore when the mall opened. I wrote to ask for an application (all this before the retirement date) and started the ball rolling towards a new job and a change of pace. I was *being the change I wanted to see happen.*

It wasn't easy to just relax and flow with the situation. Anxiety took over sometimes as I did *need* the job. But knowing that if it was the right way to go, all would work out, I *let go of all expectations and lived instead in abundant expectancy.* Step by step I *created a new reality consciously.* The job became mine, with just enough hours and income to meet my needs and help keep me in touch with people, yet allowing enough leisure to pursue many other interests.

I put a new set of tires on the slightly-used chassis and now go spinning along at the wheel, growing and living and loving it. Retirement became a challenge, a beginning, a continuing, a living with love, anticipating the future. I *create my own reality, consciously* by actively *choosing* the best kind of tires for the wheels of the rest of my life.

Dottie Wiles
Redding, CA

Loving While at Work

Picture three women working together in rather close quarters for six years. They had been through many things together, both sad and happy; yet, you can rest assured that there were many opportunities to practice the **Love Project** principles, particularly when there was a great deal of friction between two of them, not usually on the surface, but always waiting to erupt. To get the picture straight, I'm one of the two. Recently, because of tragic circumstances, the neutral one in the middle chose to take sides, adding considerably to the tension.

Up until this point, I really tried to practice the principle of *receiving all people as beautiful exactly where they are.* I had a very difficult time, because each time that I thought I was succeeding and that I was *being the change I wanted to see happen*—i.e., creating a pleasant, cooperative atmosphere in spite of the actual work tension—the volcano would erupt and we were back where we started.

Last spring when the third party involved, namely B., turned against me, my little self took over completely. I was in a total nervous state, I was barely functioning at work, making lots of mistakes and feeling totally inadequate and very hurt. I suddenly realized that I, who loved going to work every morning, now hated the thought of it.

One morning on my way to work, I literally told my little self to step aside. She had been running things long enough and it was time for my Higher Self to take over and consciously live the **Love Project** principles. I decided that I didn't have to love M., but I could still *receive her as beautiful—where she is*. This was my first step. I had *no expectations*—I was literally fighting for my life—but I had *abundant expectancy* that I could *be the change*.

At this time, when we were terribly overloaded with work, a new project was given to us: we must keep track of our time. How do you do this when you are doing deversified work? I thought about it and decided that this was an *opportunity, not a problem*. I would keep an accurate log of my time and I would *consciously create the reality of some changes*— less work and more space. During the few weeks that we were working on this schedule, we had a change in personnel—a new controller, who had worked with M. and knew her well. Naturally, he had planned to make some changes, and when he saw my work schedule and we discussed the situation, it made his plans more realistic.

Because of other changes in the upper echelon, there was an office available which he was able to give to me, and my work load was cut. I am still very busy and still under pressure at times, but also very happy. The three of us are on good terms. Our work is inter-related, so practicing the principles is now becoming an ongoing, daily part of my life. The result is that the word hostility has in all cases been replaced by consideration of one another.

Elsie Daly,
Canoga Park, CA

Practicing The Love Project Principles

With the passage of time I have become aware of discernible changes which have taken place with me, and from my viewpoint they have been welcome and for the best. The focal point of the pleasantry of this very much enriched life lies in my recognition of caring and sharing.

Awareness and practice have been of incalculable importance. As a general rule, I still believe that no one really plans to be rude or offensive by premeditation or inborn design. That is to say, you don't awaken in the morning and say to yourself "Today I am going to make everyone's life miserable."

But what a difference it makes if you begin each day with the conscious thought of how you are going to apply the principles of **The Love Project.**

From the first, when I began to *receive people as beautiful where they are,* my relationshp to others took giant steps forward. No more pretensions on my part that the other person was different than what I beheld. They are they, and once I accepted them as they are—they really are beautiful. By adhering to this principle, *expectations* were replaced by *abundant expectancy.*

There is a correlation between the **Love Project** principles and adherence to the Golden Rule. In each instance, the mind rejects any intrusions which would make you act contrary to your conscience. Self-centeredness is replaced by receiving and sharing.

The nature of my work, for more years than I care to remember, placed me in the position where any decisions I made were irrevocable. This was and is an awesome role. Applying the **Love Project** principles, especially *turning problems into opportunities,* has been the turning point of my business life. Solving a problem in which dictatorial thinking is replaced by solutions in which all persons involved are gainers, even if in unequal proportions, has made the much needed transformation in my life.

I am most grateful to my wife, Elsie, who introduced me to the **Love Project** principles. My resistance to them was replaced by enthusiasm, and automatically when confronted with annoyance, the antidote is applying the principle which best suits the circumstances.

The **Love Project** principles work. Try it—you'll like it.

David Daly,
Canoga Park, CA

Redefining Family Ties and Relationships

My consciousness in relation to myself and my family began to expand with my return to San Francisco State in 1963 to pursue a graduate degree in counseling. As a middlescent flower-child amidst the exciting and turbulent freedom movement, I returned to campus for retread, for nurturing not found in my traditional roles. The graduate counseling program was a perfect small workshop for aiding my own personality-psyche cleanup. Carl Rodgers and Abraham Maslow were pointing a new direction for freeing human potential in what was called a Third Force Humanistic Psychology approach to life and relationships.

At the same time, my spiritual involvement was accelerating. As one of a small circle of women, I went into the black community as a volunteer teacher aide and counselor in order to help create a larger circle of reality than my privilged, suburban, lily-white community had offered me. We cooperated with children in choosing activities through which they could grow, helping, too, to sharpen their skills. We started an interracial circle for parents that eventually expanded into our church family.

I had long had a larger vision of universal family and brotherhood relationships buried deep within me, and that vision began to be nurtured and affirmed in new ways. Various group processes allowed me to experience open, honest, and expansive communication that I had never known. I was part of the changes in attitude and behaviour that allowed for close and loving relationships between persons so different as to 'blow' all my old models. I was learning to *provide others with opportunitites to give* to me in ways that expanded my reality enormously.

Now I wanted to *be the change, to create a new reality,* at all levels of my life, especially with family and friends. But, I neglected *no expectations* and *receiving people just where they were*. Many with whom I desired most to communicate and be understood seemed to become more rigid and closed. I felt separated, as I sensed people saw me as threatening, too far-out, a middle-aged hippie, unappreciative and destructive of my 'good life.' Meanwhile, in my other world I experienced being a new-born, curious child. The transition was painful and confusing as idealized

184

old models of 'One Man's Family' image and 'the family that prays together, stays together,' exploded and disintegrated.

At all levels the dying began, as did the miracles. I was discovering that *problems are opportunities.* I became clearer in my commitment to my God- self. I learned that God does work in small and obscure ways.

In the late 1960's, I became parent to an emotionally and physically ill father, as well as comforter and confidant to a devastated and terminally ill favorite aunt. By engaging openly with the realities of both Dad and his sister in a step by step process, I was able to help both to welcome death as rebirth and graduation. An I could see how leaving the body was akin to the many forms of dying I was experiencing in giving up old thought forms for new ones.

An even more radical change in family and friendship connection took place with my husband's sudden death in 1969. My family roles were gone with only a fourteen year old daughter at home. My support and nurturing continued to come from group explorations where many methods, techniques, and tools for self-growth were practiced. Each new relationship and experience was a mirror to purify my image. The big awakening came with seeing All as One, and I began to *create my new reality* in a broader consciousness.

I sold the family home to buy my first home alone. In order fully to *be the change I wanted to see happen,* I released old family holiday traditions, celebrations, vacations. I *provided my family with opportunities to give* of their unique selves to me, and new patterns began to develop between my mother, daughters, friends and me. We were each moving toward more independence, freeing energy to be used in our lives 'now.' Less and less 'duty doing' and involvement in each others' *problems* illumined how 'helping' often interferes with another's process by confusing, fragmenting, and dissipating the *opportunity* for growth.

I had lost sight of the quest to know Self in the confusion of conforming temporarily to family, school, and societal programming. However, even that was perfect and I came to be able to *receive myself and others as beautiful where we had been as well as where we are.* With *no expectations* but *abundant expectancy*, I accepted the challenge of self-transformation and *made the choice* to become one of God's mirrors as I travel back to membership in His Family.

The Love Project has become in large part my Earth family. During three travel trips and in many practice sessions, six simply stated principles have been guides for fellow travelers to act as multifaceted learning mirrors for each other. Universal family ties untie, expand, and transform, rather than conform.

Flowing in the process for six glorious years has returned me to knowing more 'who I am.' I *choose* to be a bridge and connecter for New Age transition into a changed universal order. Expanding souls are evolving, spiraling, and uniting with similar soul energy vibrations in order to rebalance and connect all life on this planet to a Universal Oversoul. I *choose* this connection for my family in love, peace, harmony, cooperation and joy.

Anita Pitcher,
Tiburon, CA

Starting a New Life

Just after Christmas 1972 as we were fast approaching our 25th anniversary, my husband, to my dismay, asked me not to celebrate, but to separate! To his surprise, and *mine*, within six weeks I had made a decision to leave our home in New York, had packed a few things in the trunk of my car, and had driven to California to begin a new life.

Except that I knew it was near San Francisco, I had no conception of Marin County nor any previous connection there, but one phone call from New York had opened the door to a lovely place for me to live upon my arrival. I had *provided others, even strangers, with an opportunity to give,* and I was graciously received. Since that time in early 1973, I have been continually amazed and delighted that the new home I instinctively chose for myself is the over-the-rainbow place called Marin. I have *consciously created the reality* of living in a paradise on earth. I now realize I was practicing **Love Project** principles before I had heard them by that name. Faith in the infinite goodness and expanding possibilites of Life, by any other name works just the same!

Meanwhile, my little self was going through an enormous amount of pain when I arrived here in the midst of what the locals called winter, but to me was a miracle of springtime, all golden with acacia against a profusion of greens. Within me, a terrible winter had just begun. Separation from my beloved husband sent me into oceans of grief, and excruciating withdrawal symptoms. I was acutely addicted to that man! There was outrage at the mutilation of the beautifully woven fabric of our relationship, so long and lovingly in the making.

Yet, despite my emotional reaction, at the spiritual level of my being I was able to *receive my husband as beautiful just where he was,* for in pursuing his own process he was being the catalyst for mine. I knew it, my anguished protest notwithstanding. He was the instrument of a new birth, pushing me away from my known and visible security into an unknown assurance—a necessary stage of growth and maturing which I could not, or would not, have voluntarily initiated for myself.

My sense of personal loss and rejection by my husband were very real—another *reality which I was consciously creating* in order to face it and move through it—but I refused to reject *myself.* I could *receive myself as beautiful* in the audacity and courage, the clear integrity with which I was meeting this evolutionary crisis in my life. I was birthing myself in the midst of the death of all that I had cherished for so long.

Now past fifty, the *problem* of being alone and on my own with virtually no financial underpinnings is *providing an opportunity* to practice a direct, intimate relationship with the true Source, trusting day by day, year by year, that my needs—not necessarily my wants, but my real needs—are being met. And they are. Perfectly.

Also, the *problem* of being cast on my own is an *opportunity* to explore new ways of being, new patterns of 'home' and 'family.' I live now in a sharing, caring arrangement with two other women, and my 'extended family' are the members of the supportive community that I have been a part of since my first days in Marin. My *problem has been an opportunity* to plumb new dimensions of myself through outlets for which there was neither time nor energy in the years of homemaking and mothering. In early 1974 I returned to

187

college after a thirty-year hiatus. My youngest son used to say to me, "Mom, what are you going to be when you grow up?" I was finally on my way to finding out.

Being ever more in tune with my Higher Self, my old fears and ego needs have largely dropped away. I am again a child in the loving embrace of my Heavenly Father. *This awareness has freed me to meet life situations without preconceived **expectations**, but with a certain naivete and innocence which is childlike in its **abundant expectancy**.* I am rarely, if ever, disappointed. My non-expectation return to school blossomed gently and non-stressfully into graduation in 1976 with a degree in Expressive Arts. The experience validated my talent as a writer and the value of my life experience as the subject of my writing. My work is more and more distilling itself into poetry, as evidence of the cleansing, purification process through which I have come.

There is still a bit of nostalgia for that family that I loved so much, and who now seem so dispersed. But there is also compensation in the separate individual relationships which have developed with my four sons. Each is *beautiful just where he is*. I am no longer mother as much as peer and friend. I *provided them the opportunity to give* me encouragement and enthusiasm for my new life, and they do. It is obvious they are proud of me.

What I have always wanted and encouraged my sons to do, I am doing in my own life. I am being true to my Self. Listening, trusting, the whispers of my Soul, I am ever guided to that Eternal Home where my destiny is realized in joyous union with the true bridegroom, the Cosmic Christ. *I am being the change I want to see happen.*

Lucille Barru,
Marin County, CA

Learning from Cancer

Over seven years ago I had a breast removed because of cancer. It was a devastating blow. It wrenched my world upside down. I felt lost in a sea of fear. But it was in the coping with that crisis which has struck to the very core of my being that I began my life's most valuable experience.

Gradually, and ever so slowly at first, I began to *perceive this problem as an opportunity.* Here was an opportunity to discover the potential of the 'real me;' here was the opportunity to perceive this event as a message from my Higher Self. What could I learn from having cancer?

One of the first things I learned was that my emotions did not have to make sense. They had a right to be. Somehow, early in life, my rational self in order to stay in control had convinced me that my powerful, threatening feelings must be repressed. Three weeks after my surgery, my body was manifesting many symptoms of this repressed solar plexus energy. My stomach ached and felt like it was tied in a knot; I wheezed and couldn't breathe; I cried all the time. My doctor wisely urged, "Let your feelings out, express your emotions." I chose to do this, to *be the change I want to see happen.* For half an hour, with my feeling-self in one chair, my rational-self in another chair and my observer-self listening to both, with great sobs I expressed feelings of fear, of pain, of losing control, of dying, feelings of anger, outrage, grief, a sense of betrayal. Afterwards I experienced such a release, such relief— the life-energy was flowing again! I was *receiving myself as beautiful right where I was.* It was OK to feel!

Some time after the surgery I had an opportunity to hear Dr. Carl Simonton, a specialist in Oncology and Radiology, who was combining conventional medical treatment with psychotherapy and a visualization process designed to enhance the effectiveness of the body's immune system. After the cancer had metastasized, I began doing the relaxations and visualization process with great gratitude that I *provided Carl Simonton with the opportunity to give to me.* It felt so good to be able to do something to cooperate with the body's healing energies.

I made other lifestyle changes. I began *creating my own reality consciously.* Deliberately, by choice, I tuned into my own Inner Being and sought to align my thoughts, feelings and physical body with Its highest purpose. I became more aware of my body's needs as I experimented in changing my nutrition, using mega vitamins, shiatsu massage, meditation and relaxation. I had many psychosynthesis sessions to discover the emotional blocks preventing the free flowing of life and heart energy. I examined my beliefs and attitudes. I had *abundant expectancy and no expectations* of how all of these methods would combine with the chemotherapy to bring me into remission.

I was in remission for almost two years after stopping the chemotherapy. Then I had a regrowth and with it came feelings of recrimination and guilt instigated by my inner critic. "What are you doing wrong, Milly, to make the cancer grow again? Why can't you be an example of Holistic Health? Why aren't you good enough?" I struggled with this—I was *not receiving myself as beautiful right where I was.* Also, I found myself clinging desperately to the visualization process; it became my god. I had many *expectations* about what it *had* to do for me.

Then a weekend with **The Love Project** became a special *opportunity for others to give to me.* In a profound dialogue with my Higher Self I experienced such acceptance, such love, no condemnation; I was *being received as beautiful right where I was!* It seemed the message from the Higher Self was that going through this experience was part of what I was choosing in manifesting through my personality. Having cancer was temporary and it was OK for me to be there!

From that perspective I was able again to let go of the *expectations* I had placed on the visual imagery process and to have *abundant expectancy* that my body knows how to do its own healing. Yes, I still visualize the immune system working, but with love and deep appreciation for the body's wisdom while also allowing the immune system—or whatever—to heal in ways I am not aware of.

Today I am aware that my encounter with cancer has been a tremendous learning experience. It is a lesson in learning to BE. I am *consciously choosing* each moment to BE the Soul, the Higher Self, and to express and manifest my Self through my body, emotions and intellect. *I am being the change I want to see happen.* I am *creating my own reality consciously.* I am Life and Love and expressing that in my body, in my family relationships, in my counseling and in my service to Humanity.

Again this morning I was intensely aware of the life energy and the love flowing through me. I experienced it deep within my cells, harmonizing and transforming. It occurred to me that in the flow of that transforming energy, those cancer cells could be changed into whole, healthy, normal, vibrant cells, radiant with that life energy/love. In changing form, some cancer cells may die and others be transformed to a higher level of purpose. Death and rebirth are part of the change process. Letting go of the old and welcoming of the new is part of the *reality I am creating consciously.* I am Life!

Milly Collinsworth,*
Fresno, CA

A Changing Life Style

Today we hear a lot of talk about the tragedy of divorce. It is scary and sad to change your lifestyle after fifteen years. But for me the largest *problem* of my life has been the biggest *opportunity for growth* yet.

Receiving all persons as beautiful exactly where they are felt impossible when my husband told me that he was in love with a man. I don't know when I've cried so hard. I was angry at society in general for not accepting homosexuality. I felt people were forced to marry to be accepted by society, parents, etc.

The greatest gift of love I've ever given was releasing my husband to be himself. I couldn't do anything about society and its attitude, but I could *be the change I wanted to see happen* by *receiving him as beautiful exactly where he is,* even though I would have much rather had him in a different place.

Even though I felt that I had no control over my life at that point, I was handed an opportunity to *create my own reality* like never before.

For me, being married restricted my relationships with other people, especially men. I was in pain and feeling very unfeminine. With *no expectations,* I phoned a man that I felt very comfortable talking with, and told him that when he was in the area, I really needed a friend to talk with. Taking a chance of being rejected, I *provided him with an opportunity to give* me what I needed most in life at that

---

*Milly died in April, 1979 before this book was published. We are grateful for her life and her shining witness to the power of love.

191

moment. It wasn't a shoulder to cry on, it was someone who would listen without judging. I knew he was attracted to me, and as I look back on that first phone call I was also asking to be loved and made to feel feminine again.

Having no expectations, I never dreamed that he would take a day off work and fly down to talk with me. He didn't have any idea what I wanted. He just came. What a beautiful gift of love he gave to me by not only not rejecting me but by making me feel that I was more important than his work (the love of his life.)

Our friendship grew into a beautiful love affair which was a *conscious choice* that we both made. We are still very close and no one can ever take away the love we shared.

Later, I had a party which seemed like a huge *problem.* A single lady giving a party in a couples' world (the majority of friendships I'd made while married were also married) was so frightening. Believe me, I had *no expectations but rather abundant expectancy* and butterflies in my stomach when the party began. That evening provided me with an *opportunity* to be more extroverted because I was not overshadowed or dependent on a husband or date. I was able to enjoy each person more fully and to be totally myself.

It was probably no accident that my husband and I were together in this life, because we both are now expressing parts of ourselves that are unorthodox according to society's rules. It was harder for me to *receive* that unorthodox part of myself *as beautiful* than it was to *receive* my husband.

Because I am now *receiving my unorthodox self as beautiful* I am able to open up the book of my life for each person to look at and decide where my pain and joy triggers a reaction in his or her own life.

I had a beautiful relationship with a married teacher at my children's school. We *provided each other with the opportunity* to love at the expense of being rejected by many people in the community. It was very hard for me to *receive these people as beautiful* until I realized they were reacting from their own insecurities about their own marriages. I can understand and love them, but I cannot have my life ruled by their rules.

As I look back on that *problem*, it was just a stepping stone of *growth* for the relationship I am in today. He is black.

and I white. I am *being the change I want to see happen* by simply enjoying our relationship. I'm *receiving all persons as beautiful* no matter what their reaction. I realize how difficult it is not to react to feelings that have been handed down from generation to generation.

We are both *providing our friends with the opportunity to love us* for ourselves, with *no expectations but rather abundant expectancy.* They have received us and loved us and slowly erased many of their own prejudices.

I am *creating my own reality* by being an example to my children that I can love each person because no one has control over my life except me. This *problem has definitely been an opportunity for me to grow.*

A Los Angeles **Seeker**

Chapter Ten
THE LOVE PROJECT WAY

There comes a point in the cosmic process of individualization when each of us seeks to consciously cooperate with, and thus to speed up, our evolutionary unfoldment into self-realization. When we reach that point, we seek a 'way,' a 'path,' which will facilitate our growth and our awakening. We want to know how we can more quickly attain that which will ultimately satisfy all our longings, give us inner peace, universal understanding and hearts filled with love for all humankind. We seek to know ourselves, others, and the universe around us. We seek to know total union, within and without.

Sometimes we have been raised within a religious tradition that meets our needs at that crucial phase of our unfoldment and serves naturally and easily for us as our 'way.' But sometimes the religion in which we were raised does not seem adequate, or we have not been raised with a religious background at all. In those cases we look elsewhere for guidance and direction.

In the Eastern spiritual traditions there is a saying: "When the disciple is ready, the teacher will appear." A 'teacher' is one who will show you a way—the way he or she has walked and thus knows intimately, trusts totally, and knows will take you to your goal because it has taken him/her to his/hers.

Teachers abound. Paths abound. In order to find *your* path, and to decide whether this teacher or that is one from whom you can learn how to most quickly reach your goal, you must rely on your own inner voice, the 'teacher' within you, your own Higher Self. This is as it should be, for when that sense of urgency arises within you and you long to find a teacher who can show you your way, you are already responding to the teacher within you. Your responsiveness to your inner voice prompts you to seek an outer echo for that voice. What you seek is someone to confirm for you that you are on your way and to mirror-reflect for you your own process of awakening to what you already know but have forgotten and are now ready to remember again.

As you seek your own path then, you must rely solely on inner guidance to determine which ways most clearly approximate *your* way. You will feel yourself drawn to these paths, and to the teachers that represent those paths. You will feel at home with them on deep levels of your inner being, even if the outer expression of the path is 'foreign' to you in light of your experiences thus far in your life. You will trust the paths and the teachers because they will be in harmony with your own inner knowing. And you will also know when and if it is no longer in harmony for you to follow a given path or to learn from a certain teacher, for your own restlessness and inner prompting will tell you to "move on."

Making a 100% Commitment

It is important, when you are ready to cooperate consciously with your own evolution and thus to hasten your process of self-realization, that you make a total commitment of your energies to a 'way.' You make this commitment, not because that way is the *only* way, but because you are choosing it as *your* way, and it cannot be your way unless you walk it with the whole of your being. If you are headed to a mountain top, it will take you much longer to get there if you keep walking *around* the mountain, trying first one path and then another. That kind of sampling and testing and tasting is important in the beginning, while you are looking for your path. Once you have found one which is in harmony with you, however, it is important to start toward the top, not dissipating your energy further with side tracks.

This does not mean, of course, that the things you have learned before starting on a given path, and what you will continue to learn from reading of and talking to others who are walking other paths, will not inform and enrich your journey. It simply means that you will make a commitment to let your energies flow 100% in one direction, that you have decided to make a concerted effort to get to the top. All other data and

195

information you take in will strengthen you for your journey and heighten your awareness along the way, but you will continue on the same path until you reach the peak. This is what choosing a path means.

Once you have chosen a path, every experience you have along the way and every person you meet will be an opportunity for you to learn what you need to learn in order to reach the 'top.' You may have several teachers along the way, each of whom will help you along a particular portion of the path. Some teachers may stay with you for the entire journey. Your experience in this regard will be different from anyone else's, for this is *your* journey on the path, and your teacher within will guide you through whatever reflections of your inner knowing you recognize as you go along.

Any commitment you make to a Way is between you and your Higher Self or inner teacher. Only you can know if you have made a 100% commitment or choice, and only you can sustain it. Any outer teachers you relate to will mirror-reflect only what you have first set in motion from within.

When you are ready, and when you have made your choice of a pathway—one which is in harmony for you—then your *real* search begins, your search for your essential self, the knowing of your divine perfection and of your harmony with the cosmic plan. The path is the journey you take. The mountain is as high as you perceive the journey to be difficult. The peak is the discovery of your real self, for you are already there.

The Love Project as a Way

The Love Project was not originally given as a way *to* enlightenment, but rather as a way of living out the wisdom and inner knowing the authors had each come to by walking diverse paths. Each of us independently broke through to cosmic consciousness and remembered our divine heritage as our natural right, and the six principles were given as a simple and profound summary of the wisdom we came to see and as aids to the process of integrating that profound inner knowing into the living of our everyday lives. They were the means of being and doing what we saw we were: divine beings in manifestation.

When we began sharing these principles with others, therefore, it did not occur to us that we were offering a 'way,' a 'path.' All we knew was that these principles worked for us in enabling us to live in the peace, oneness and joy that is promised to all who know the One, and that they were gifts which it was our joy to pass on.

Over the years, however, as we have worked with and practiced alongside other persons, we have come to recognize the transforming power of the six **Love Project** principles. For persons who already know their oneness with God, the principles facilitate the process of integration of that wisdom into everyday living—the process of transformation of the personality self to bring it into total harmony with the perfect pattern being revealed step by step to and through Higher Self. For those who are *seeking* self-realization, enlightenment, cosmic union, the principles offer a very creative and practical means of preparing their vehicles for the registry in consciousness of those higher frequencies.

It seems time, then, to offer to those who seek it **The Love Project** as a way, a way we find to be very much in harmony with the vibration of the Aquarian Age. It is a way that focuses on harmony, peace and universal love—hallmarks of this age—and which stresses the importance of finding your inner authority and source of wisdom and following that without wavering, while at the same time living cooperatively and synergistically with others.

Is the Love Project Your Way?

If you seek union within yourself and with other persons and with the cosmic pattern via a pathway of love, **The Love Project** may be a way for you. The path of love is primarily a horizontal rather than a vertical path. You walk into the heart of the Universe by walking through the doorways provided by yourself and other persons. When every door is unlocked by you and to you, when you have found the passageway into and through every other being on the planet, then you will know the One who is in all, who is all, and you will love that One with all your soul and heart and mind and strength.

The pathway of love is like walking directly into and through the mountain to discover paradoxically, that when you get to the other side, you are on top, and simultaneously are where you began.

It is possible to *know*, to gain wisdom, without loving. If we do that, we have union on 'inner' planes, but are not able to manifest and experience that union in our 'outer' lives, with other persons. Such self-realization is comparable to studying piano playing and learning all *about* it without actually learning to play the piano. On the other hand, when we learn to love—self, others and the cosmos—we come to know all there is to know through our life experiences, on both inner and outer planes. The way of Love, then, is a pathway of direct experience, of wisdom gained through living, of knowledge attained simultaneously with understanding. It is a pathway for those who want to stay fully in the body, on the planet earth, while learning to live in the energy frequencies which characterize the farthest reaches of consciousness in the cosmos. It is a pathway of organic expansion from within, starting from where you are and moving step by step into the vastness of your own potential. It is a pathway of joyously grounded soaring.

The way of Love is a middle way, a way of balance. The heart chakra or energy center is the midpoint in the human energy system. When we function with our heart chakras wide open, when we live in universal love, we do so by bringing the four other chakras of manifestation (the generative, solar plexus, throat and three eyes centers) into harmony and balance and by consciously activating the polarities of universal energy (the sacral and crown chakras) in our being so that we become open and flowing channels of the Life Force in manifestation, that is, Love.

The **Love Project** principles are a 'teacher' that can show you your way if you wish to walk the path of Love. They are not the only teacher of this way, but they are a very effective one.

The principles act as your teacher by awakening in your own consciousness your knowing of what it is to live as a divine being. They are the voice of the Higher Self saying, "If you would know me, then walk with me, live with me, be one with me. Enter my energy field, be one with my pattern, experience what I know." The six **Love Project** principles are a simple statement of how the One manifests as the Many in total consonance and joy.

If you receive the **Love Project** principles as a teacher and decide to walk the way of Love to self-realization, then your own inner teacher, your Higher Self, will utilize these principles in taking you step by step along the way as you are going 'home.' The principles will serve for you as a way to focus your consciousness and quiet your objective mind so that you can more clearly hear your inner voice. They will open the door of new possiblities to you in experience after experience, thus enabling you to realize your full potential. They will take you deeper into the heart of the Universe each time you put them into practice in the actual living of your life. They will be with you constantly, for you will take them with you as you go, transforming your own way of living as you let love work in and through you.

The **Love Project** principles will show you how to live a life of service by making your own unique contribution and doing the work that you have come to do as one essential expression of the divine in manifestation. They will teach you how to be and do love under all circumstances at all levels of your being.

Making a Choice

In order to make a choice regarding a pathway, you need exposure to and experience with what that way represents. If you are new to **The Love Project** and it is new to you, we suggest you live with the principles for a while. Try them out. See if they work for you and if they are in harmony with your inner approach to life. Get acquainted with them before you decide how you want to continue to be related to them.

You may find that **The Love Project** principles are not in harmony with your approach to living and that they are not a 'teacher' you want to associate with in any way, or at least not in *every* way. We bless you on your way and delight in your clarity about the path you have *chosen* to follow. At least you know it is *not* this one!

You may not be seeking a way. If that is so, then the **Love Project** principles may serve to make your life more joyful by helping you to bring more love into it and to express more love through it to whatever degree *you choose* to activate and utilize the principles in your everyday life. We welcome your sharing in our "life with the principles" in any way and to whatever extent *you choose.*

You may have already chosen another way. If that is so, the **Love Project** principles may serve to supplement and facilitate your progress on your chosen path. They may add to what you already know and act as one more expression of the wisdom you are coming to remember. That too is beautiful, and we rejoice with you and are glad to share with you as you wish, and in whatever ways we can.

Or, you may decide that Love is your way and that you want to receive the **Love Project** principles as one teacher on that way. If so, we would like to invite you to share your decision with us,* for though the **Love Project** principles will be your teacher and you don't need anyone else for that interaction of learning and growth, nevertheless it has been our experience that it is also helpful to have mirrors to look in as you walk along your way in order to see yourself more clearly and to find your way more quickly. We offer you mirrors to look in: us, for two, and others who have chosen **The Love Project** as a way and who will be mirrors for you in their own unique ways, too. Moreover, if you share in our conscious companionship on the **Love Project** Way, you will be a mirror for others to look in to see their own perfection mirrored in your process. That is part of the service you will offer, and our own experience has been that it gives strength and encouragement to know who walks beside you.

Whatever *choice* you make, you are an important member of our Love Family and we rejoice in our oneness with you and in our opportunity to have touched lives consciously in whatever way and for whatever length of time is in harmony for us so to do.

---

*You can write to us, Diane and Arleen, at P.O. Box 7601, San Diego, CA 92107. (714) 225-0133.

Learning to Love: Horizontal Travel

If you have chosen the pathway of Love, then your primary focus from now on, will be on loving. While you will lift your eyes occasionally to catch glimpses of where you are going, it is important to realize that your primary focus will be on where you are and what next, immediate steps you will take. This is the horizontal nature of the path.

The key **Love Project** principle for this aspect of the pathway is *Receive All People As Beautiful Exactly Where They Are.* Once you choose a path and accept it as an outer reflection of the wisdom your inner teacher is revealing to you, it is easier to accept the fact that everything you encounter along the way, and everyone, is part of the learning you are doing. Whoever comes into your consciousness along the way of Love is given to you in order that you might practice loving them wholly, totally, unconditionally, universally. Whatever experience comes to you along the way of Love, no matter how difficult, is in order that you might learn to love your*self* wholly, totally, unconditionally, universally.

This universal love is most easily and readily released from within when you practice praise and thanksgiving for all things all day every day. If you will allow yourself to say, "Thank you, Father, Thank you, Mother" (a reminder that both polarities of the universal Life Force are needed to bring anything into manifestation), with enthusiasm and a sense of awe and wonder for *every* event and person that comes into your consciousness, you will find your heart center opening more and more, not only to the cosmos and that universal source of Love, but also to the persons and events themselves. It is important to offer praise and thanksgiving for *every*thing, even those events and persons you label 'bad,' or 'wrong,' 'distasteful,' 'impossible,' etc. To give thanks for them does not mean that you will not wrestle with them and suffer from them, or through them, it simply means you will all the while be grateful for the *opportunities* they represent and consciously acknowledge that you are grateful.

You may want to start each morning with this as your thought-prayer: "This is the day the Lord has made. I will rejoice and be exceedingly glad in it." Throughout the day, say (silently within, or aloud), "Thank you, Father, Thank you, Mother" for each new experience. And just before going to sleep at night, you may want to say-pray: "Father-Mother, in response to all you have already given me, I offer a thankful heart."

When your heart is filled with gratitude, you will find it much easier to practice the principle *Receive All People As Beautiful Exactly Where They Are.* Each person is on his or her own perfect path, as you are, and each one offers you a unique learning, for the Life Force comes to you in each being and speaks to you if you have ears to hear. If you have difficulty receiving persons as beautiful exactly where they are—including yourself—then there is some message you are resisting, some lesson your inner teacher is trying to call to your attention, and you will find it difficult to proceed further on your path without stumbling on this 'block' in your way. As you offer thanks for this condition within you, or characteristic or limitation or 'handicap' that you have, or this person with whom you disagree or whom you find distasteful, and open yourself more fully until you can love yourself and all others unconditionally, you will find yourself bounding along your way.

Learning Through Direct Experience

If you have chosen the pathway of Love, then you will want to leave yourself totally open and vulnerable all the time, for it is impossible to love unless you are open, and it is impossible to learn and grow unless you are vulnerable. The pathway of Love is one of learning through your direct experience what you need to know about life. Such learning cannot be found in a book. It is found in the midst of living.

Practice, therefore, staying open and vulnerable, welcoming all experiences that come your way and entering into them fully, wholeheartedly, uncompromisingly. If the experience that comes brings pain and you have difficulty with it, this is because you are putting up resistance to it and struggling against it on some level of your being. Go into the pain, and into the struggle, into the difficulty, for it is there, in the experience, that you will discover your own learning, and in that learning, your own freedom. Until you have fully entered the experience and learned all there is for you to know from it and through it, you will find it always before you, beside you or around you as you proceed along your way. It will not leave you until you have made your peace with it, learned to love yourself in and through it, and given thanks for the gifts it has brought you.

Each experience is an opportunity for you to come to know and understand all about life and the nature of the cosmos. Your inner teacher will speak to you through it. So, *Perceive Problems as Opportunities and Provide Others With Opportunities to Give to You.* Say open. Be vulnerable.

Expand From Within

It is impossible to start walking your path of Love from anywhere other than where you are. Once you have chosen your path, you must travel the entire way. You step out onto the path where you are. When you do, you will find others who are on the same path, but not all will be beginners any more than you are a beginner. It is only in your objective mind that you think you are just beginning. Actually, you have already covered a lot of territory and there is much you have learned which will return to you very quickly now that you are open to remember what you know. For others, the same is true. It is not possible to know, by virtue of being in the same time-space with someone, whether you are 'more' or 'less' advanced along the path than they are. Your learning in this lifetime is only an infinitesimal part of your total learning which is an accumulation of wisdom from a multitude of life experiences. Such is also the case for all others.

Do not try, therefore, to compare yourself with others, saying "You're more advanced than I am," or "I'm further along than you are." Instead, *Bring Into Consciousness The Reality You Have Been Creating* in order to assess where you are and how you got there. Then open yourself to what is next *for you,* and the minute you see what it is, *Be The Change You Want To See Happen* rather than wasting any time trying to change anyone else. What you see to do and be is *yours* to do and be. Someone else, though standing alongside you on the path, may have an entirely different task set before him/her for his/her own learning. Get on with your own journey. It is for each person to make his/her own.

Where you are is perfect for you. Your inner teacher has been guiding and directing your life experience, waiting for you to awaken to consciousness so that you could see all that there is for you to see. Be glad that you are where you are, and start from there. There could be no better way for you.

Balance and Harmony: The Middle Way

The pathway of Love is a middle way, a path of harmony and balance. You will make greater progress by developing all aspects of your being, opening all the energy centers, than by concentrating on any one, even the heart chakra. Balance in your being is established when there is an unblocked flow of energy from the universal Source through the crown center (the positive polarity of your energy being), down through your being to the sacral chakra (the negative polarity of your energy being) and back again to the Source (this is the 'vertical' flow in your being), and when there is an unblocked flow of energy from, through and to you through each of the five chakras of manifestation, with the heart center maintaining the balance in its universal flow of love (the 'horizontal' flow.)

Make use, then, of whatever methods and approaches are helpful to you to open yourself as an equal-armed cross of energy in the world.

The Polarities of Universal Energy: The 'Vertical' Flow

Open yourself to conscious awareness of the universal Life Force flowing through your own being. *Have No Expectations, But Rather Abundant Expectancy,* for if you live in *abundant expectancy*, then you will know that anything is possible and your future is entirely open. As you live in *abundant expectancy*, you will more and more recognize that *Choice Is The Life Process* and that you are actually

free to make new choices in every new moment of awareness. Stay open to that flow and you will begin to experience yourself as a divine being, unlimited by any condition, filled with the divine Life Force, a creator.

You may want to practice meditation as a way of learning to wait in the void, with *abundant expectancy* (being conscious, then, of the energy of the sacral chakra), and of opening yourself to unthought-of possibilities (consciousness of the energy of the crown chakra.) Choose any form of meditation that works for you. Books and teachers abound. Allow yourself to be led by your inner voice. The important thing is to learn to relax totally, to quiet your objective mind, to open your whole being to your Higher Self from which all that is new will come to you, and to channel and direct your energies.*

It is equally important to practice *letting go of expectations* and staying open to new possibilities in the midst of your activities, while practicing each of the other priniciples, so that you keep that 'vertical' energy flow going all the time and your every life experience becomes a means of knowing the universal Love Force moving in and through you more and more powerfully all the time. This is constant, ongoing meditation. Meditation while "sitting" is practice for this meditation while *doing.*

Active meditation in whatever form is practicing conscious participation in the flow of energies between the crown chakra, through which you receive the Life Force and the Power-to-Be-Conscious, and the sacral chakra, in which you ground that Life Force and activate the Power-to-Be-Manifest. In this Father-Mother polarity, the vertical energy flow of your being, lies the key to Cosmic Consciousness. *Have No Expectations But Rather Abundant Expectancy* and awareness that *Choice Is The Life Process* will facilitate your openness to this flow. When you can hold both poles of creativity in your consciousness at once, you will merge with the All and the Nothing and know your infinite, limitless nature and the joy of being one with the One.

---

*A cassette tape of guided meditations which will help you to learn to do this conscious channeling of energy is available from The Love Project, P.O. Box 7601, San Diego, CA 92107.

The Balancing Flow of Universal Energy:
The 'Horizontal' Flow

It is in and through the heart center that you will establish a flow of universal energy that will keep your being in balance in the midst of everyday life while you are expanding into Cosmic Consciousness. The energy of the heart chakra is a direct 'embodied' expression of the merging of the polarities represented by the sacral and crown chakras. The heart center, for that reason, is often called the 'seat' of the 'son' born of the Father-Mother Force in the Universe. The energy of the heart center is the 'divine' in manifestation, and to live in consciousness of this universal love energy and of its perfect flow in and through your being is to live in consciousness of your 'sonship,' of yourself as 'God' incarnate.

Practicing the principle *Receive All People As Beautiful Exactly Where They Are,* which is the active expression of unconditional love, is the way, then, to activate this consciousness in you and to become a Master of life-in-manifestation, of living as a divine being on the planet earth in a human body.

One of the most helpful exercises for the opening of the heart chakra is to practice deep breathing and the following of the breath with your consciousness. Just as in breathing you must totally relax in order to fill your lungs, being as a vessel waiting to be filled, so you empty yourself and wait to be filled by the universal Life Force. Likewise, as you must let go of the air you have received, releasing it back to the Source from which it came in order for your lungs to be cleansed and ready once more to be filled, so in living you let go of each experience, releasing all 'bonds' to the past, in order to prepare yourself for and new, the next, that which is to come. And in *receiving* self and others, you not only allow each person into your consciousness, into your life space, but you let them go in order to experience them, and you, anew in the next moment of your awareness.

Again, you may want or need to learn *how* properly to breathe deeply and consciously from teachers or books. Let yourself be led to the experiences you need. You can do conscious breathing during silent meditation, and you can do it equally well, and to your enormous benefit, in the midst of interactions throughout the day. To the degree you keep breathing deeply, to that degree you will be able to open your heart to all persons, including yourself, and to live in that flow of universal Love energy on both the vertical and the horizontal planes.

Bring Your Personality Self Into Harmony With Love

The Personality Self is the Self in Manifestation. It is the reflection on this plane of consciousness of the Higher Self, which is invisible. The Personality Self is on the All side of the polarity of All and Nothing, whereas Higher Self is on the Nothing side.

You can only know as much of the Higher Self as you are manifesting in your personality self. Therefore, if you would expand your consciousness ever more widely into the vastness of the infinite, you must also expand it ever more deeply into the depths of the finite. Coming to know yourself as a personality, as self-in-manifestation, is the way you are given to know the Lord of your being, your Higher Self, in consciousness.

Therefore, it is essential, as you walk the way of Love, to constantly bring your personality self into harmony with what you will come to know as the 'God' within you on the vertical axis of interaction with the cosmos and on the horizontal plane of interaction with the world around you. There are four principles and chakras which will facilitate this process of bringing your personality self into harmony and balance with the Love flow.

1) It is in the *Three Eyes Center* that you see yourself and thus come to know yourself consciously. As you learn to *Create Your Own Reality Consciously*, you will see more and more clearly how you can *be* all that you know is possible for you to be.

To practice this principle and consciously activate the energy of the *Three Eyes Center,* therefore, it is important to:

a) Train your objective mind. Teach it to obey your consciousness rather than trying to control your life. Learn to use it effectively in the myriad of ways it can serve you so well: for reasoning, for memory, for analysis, for discrimination, for exercising judgment for the living of your own life, for weighing and assessing values, for making decisions. If you find yourself less than confident about your ability to function in any of these mental capacities, find your way to classes and/or books that will help you to awaken your potential and activate your consciousness of your mental powers.

b) Learn to quiet your mind. When you have trained your mind to do what it can do so flawlessly, then you must also train it *not* to do when you wish it to be still. There is a mode of functioning in the objective mind when the mind serves only as a mirror. Its surface is as smooth as a totally placid lake on a sunlit day when the stillness of the air enables you to see right to the bottom with absolute ease and to see a perfect reflection of all that is around and above the lake.

When you are wanting to be conscious of the 'vertical' flow of energy through your being, you will want your objective mind to be in this still mode. Then you will be able to see to the depths and heights of your being with clarity and to recognize the reflective quality of your personality self (which is analogous to the water in the lake.) It is only when your mind is still, like such a lake, that you can see clearly and gain understanding.

Many methods of meditation are addressed to this quieting of the mind, but remember that unless coupled with the training of the right use of the mind, the quieting of it will be far more difficult.

c) Learn to be conscious of your own process. Your consciousness is, as it were, the surface of the lake. In order to see into the depths, you will need to quiet the surface, to still the clamor of 'automatic thinking' which amounts to the constant playing of old tapes, either of your own making or as 'recorded' from others. Most of what we think about in the course of the day is useless. It serves no practical purpose. We are simply running over and over again thoughts we have thought before or conversations we have had with others. Once registered, a thought is recorded forever in your memory bank. There is no need to keep reinforcing it. Bring it up again only when it will be useful to you.

Your mental energies can more beneficially be put to use in process observation in the course of the day. Watch what you are doing, how you are feeling, what you are saying, even what you are thinking. Do not judge. Just watch. Allow into consciousness your own processes of interaction, of living, for it is the total configuration of those processes that make up your personality self. Only as you become aware of the patterns you have already developed will you be in a position to make any new *choices* and thus bring anything new into being in and through you.

d) Give your objective mind new data to work with. This data will come through new experiences—those you have yourself, those others tell you of, and those you read about. Expose yourself to as much newness as you can, and thereby expand the boundaries of the *reality* you live in.

e) Develop an expansive and expanding world view. You will want to listen to, talk with and read the thoughts of persons who have touched Cosmic Consciousness and are living it out in their daily lives. There are more and more such persons all the time, and there have been such persons all through history. They are not just persons known as 'religious' or 'spiritual.' They are enlightened beings, 'geniuses' in all fields of endeavor. Reading Richard Maurice Bucke's book *Cosmic Consciousness** will give you a feeling for what to look for, and/or *The Imprisoned Splendor*** by Raynor C. Johnson and *The Nature of Human Consciousness****, edited by Robert E. Ornstein will perhaps open new perceptual doors. In each of those books you will find more references to other books that you might possibly want to follow up on, and that is good. Read only what you feel drawn to. Follow your inner guidance.

The important thing is to expand your own world view, the *reality* you live within, so that you have room for anything and everything you may be exposed to on 'inner' and 'outer' planes of awareness.

2) It is in the *Solar Plexus* that you will experience the impact of your own thoughts and actions, for this is your feeling center. As you open yourself to experience more and more, you will want to feel more and more deeply all the polarities of responses available to you that you might have the total experience of life-in-manifestation.

If you will remember that *Problems are Opportunities*, then you will not close yourself to the difficult experiences of

---

*E.P. Dutton, 1964
**Harper & Row, 1953
***W.C. Freeman & Co., 1968

life, but rather you will welcome them as you welcome the easy and pleasant experiences. In fact, you will discover that here, as in all other aspects of life, only to the degree you allow yourself to experience the unpleasant will you experience more of the pleasant, and vice versa, for we expand in both directions at once in order to remain whole.

As you welcome all experiences, and give thanks for all, you will find that the joy of cosmic consciousness will be present with you through even the most painful and difficult times, and that your love-flow will expand throughout *all* that you experience.

In order to activate the energies of the *Solor Plexus* and to respond to all experiences as **opportunities**, you will want to become as a little child in relation to life: open, vulnerable, resilient, responsive. Get to know the child that you were and have been in order to release the spontaneous child you are capable of being. Again, any person, book or experience that will help you to know your inner child will help in your unfoldment in this area of your being.

3) In the *Throat Center*, you learn to verbalize your experiences as a personality self and your insights gained through Higher Self. These verbalizations are brought into form in thoughts but are only expressed when those thoughts are written down or spoken, and it is through such expression that we **Provide Others With Opportunities To Give.**

By expressing ourselves, we open the inner world of our private reality to other persons and invite them to participate in that world with us. We open ourselves to receive the gift that the other, any other, represents and brings to us in his/her unique being. To the degree we do not share what is going on 'inside' of us, to that degree we close others out. The more we share of our own experience, the more we invite others in.

Therefore, practice writing and talking about your experiences as often and fully as you can. Share of yourself with others. Open yourself to them. Give the gift of the fruits of your inner life, of your self-understanding. And then stay open to receive in return what they offer of their own experiences, of their unique offering of self to you.

4) In the *Generative Center*, you have the ability to give form to your energies on the 'physical' plane. As you activate these energies, you have the opportunity to **Be The Change**

You Want To See Happen in the world. You will bring your wisdom, understanding and insights into being through your own actions and through the products of your creative activity.

It is important not just to see, to understand, to think and talk about, or even to feel, but also to *do*. Only as you are actively doing what you are being will you bring total balance to your personality self. Find a creative outlet—or several such— into which you can pour your energies and watch something specific and concrete emerge. The energies you set in motion and to which you give form through your creative activity are an important part of the gift you give, of the service you render. The answer to the question, "What am I to do with my life?" is discovered in the doing. When you find an activity, a work, which is all-consuming of your creative energies, and to which you are eager to give all you can give, then you will have discovered your dharma, your work. But this you will find *only* by doing, not by some revelation, for it is as you see it come into form, into being, that you know: "This is it."

To activate these four principles of manifestation is to know yourself as creator, as one made in the image of The Creator. The more you come to know yourself as one who brings life into manifestation, creating realities, feeling the impact of those realities, bringing them into form and then sharing those creations with others, the more you will discover your oneness with all others who are engaged in the same life-process. You will come to know yourself to be one with the One, this time through the Many.

Companions on the Way

We offer ourselves as companions along the **Love Project** Way. We are willing to share with you.

a) by our example. We offer ourselves as living illustrations of persons who live by the **Love Project** principles and make them work in our lives. By watching us, relating to us and interacting with us, you will see how *we* walk this path of Love. Your own walking will be clarified by your similarities and contrasts with ours.

b) by reflecting on our own life process. We will be open about our inner processes—the *how* of our living—both in

212

writing and as we talk with you and others. We do not like to deal in the abstract and the theoretical, but prefer instead to give specific and concrete examples of how the **Love Project** principles work for us. As we understand it, perfection lies in *doing* the life process. We will be totally enlightened when we are totally conscious of the life process we are engaged in. We practice being more and more conscious by sharing whatever we are aware of, conscious of, in our own processes.*

c) by being your peers. We acknowledge you as having equal standing with ours in the universe. You are just as important as we are to the whole—no more and no less. Therefore, we stand beside you in joy.

d) by being mirrors for you to look in. To the degree you see your inner teacher reflected in us, to that degree you will learn from us. But always your learning will be from yourself through us. You will alter your consciousness and transform your life by the same universal grace that we are changing and expanding ours—that of the universal Life Force moving in and through you as it moves in and through us. You may see your process of transformation mirrored in us, and if so that is beautiful. We seek only to be as clear as we can so that the image you see of yourself in us will be as little distorted as possible.

e) by receiving you as our companion on the Way. All that we have said about what we are willing to be to you, we receive you as being for us: an example of one living by the principles, a reflector on your own life processes, a peer, and a mirror for us to look in to see our inner teachers reflected. What we are to you we see you as being to us, and we receive you in that spirit. We also invite you to *create consciously the reality* of what it means for you to be our campanion on the Way, and a companion to others.

Two By Two

Upon request, we will send the names and addresses of others who have committed themselves to the Way of Love and

---

*To learn more about the publications and practice sessions of **The Love Project** write to us for information at P.O. Box 7601, San Diego, CA 92107.

to the **Love Project** principles as a 'teacher' along that Way.* It is our hope that you will find companionship among these persons, that there may even emerge for you one with whom you can "go forth two-by-two," as living expressions of Love in action. It has been our experience that to have another to walk beside in consciousness as you serve is to heighten your growth in consciousness immeasurably. Though we *have no expectations,* it is our hope that some of you may find an 'other' to walk beside more closely than you can walk with all who are companions on the Way. We urge you to open yourself with *abundant expectancy* to that possibility and to the form your life of service two-by-two might take.

Our Love Family

We also invite you to be related in consciousness, and in whatever active ways you choose, to our larger Love Family. These are persons who have expressed some interest in **The Love Project** and who stay in touch with us through our *Newsletter*, our Practice Sessions, and our books. More and more these persons are learning to love each other, and many others, by practicing being loving with one another. We invite you to facilitate that experience of being members of a universal love family.

One active way you might relate is by reflecting on your experiences of growth in and through the *Seeker Newsletter*. By sharing insights you have come to through your experiences in applying the principles, you will open new doors to other **Seekers** as well as sharpening your own awareness.

Another active way you might relate is by participating in **Love Project** practice sessions, thus coming to know and to share with other **Seekers.**

You may also want to stay in touch with other **Seekers** by mail, on the phone, or in person.

And you may invent a multitude of ways to be of service to members of this Love Family by giving unique gifts of yourself.

---

*Write to us at P.O. Box 7601, San Diego, CA 92107.

Summary Suggestions For Those Walking the Love Project *Way.*

1) Live the **Love Project** principles, all day, each day.
2) Give praise and thanksgiving for all things and all people all day long each day.
3) Be totally open and vulnerable to every life experience.
4) Always start from where you are, in your perfection.
5) Bring the Life Energy Flow in your being into balance.
6) Reread this book periodically.
7) Be a companion on the Way to other **Seekers** who are walking the **Love Project** Way.
8) Be a conscious, active, response-able member of our Universal Love Family of **Seekers.**
9) Make of your life a living **Love Project** by giving of your unique creative gifts in service to others.

Chapter Eleven
CHOICE IS THE LIFE PROCESS

How you live your life, how you experience life, is the result of *choices* you have been making. Until now many of those *choices* may have been unconscious. A majority may date back to your childhood when, under the strong influence of your parents and other authority figures, you made choices that established many of the basic patterns that characterize your personality self.

But this is a new moment in time for you, and *in every new moment of awareness, you are free to make a new choice.* If you want to be in Love and to live in Love for the rest of your life, you can so choose.

A *choice* is larger than a decision. A decision is a mental affirmation of some planned course of action. However, if your feelings are not in harmony with the decision you make, you will find it difficult, if not impossible, to act upon it.

A *choice* represents a shift throughout your entire energy field. When you choose, you move with your whole self into the new represented by that *choice.* To choose is to change.

We have shared with you here a way of life that has brought joy and wholeness and balance to many, and that has set universal Love in motion in and through the lives of those who have chosen to be and do the **Love Project** principles. You may now want to make some new *choices* for your life. We hope you will choose Love, but we *have no expectations* and *receive you as beautiful* whatever you choose.

We are in Love. We love you. Do you choose Love?